PRACTICE MANAGEMENT HANDBOOK

January 1998

Personal Education Plans

LIZ Educational Incentives

Ealing, Hammersmith and Hounslow
London Initiative Zone Educational Incentives

PRACTICE MANAGEMENT HANDBOOK

Peter Forster

Industrial Relations Officer
British Medical Association North West Office
Manchester

BMJ
Publishing
Group

First published in 1995
by the BMJ Publishing Group, BMA House, Tavistock Square,
London WC1H 9JR

British Library Cataloguing in Publication Data

A catalogue record for this book is available
from the British Library

ISBN 0-7279- 0878-2

Typeset in Great Britain by Apek Typesetters Ltd., Nailsea, Bristol
Printed and bound in Great Britain by Latimer Trend & Co, Plymouth

Contents

Introduction

Recent changes in general practice and the NHS have changed the face of practice management. No longer just an administrator outside the mainstream of NHS management, today's practice manager is much more in the textbook mould of management and crucial to the future success of general practice.

Assessing healthcare needs, contracting for the provision and purchase of health services on behalf of patients, and marketing services in a competitive (albeit managed) NHS environment requires from today's practice manager the full range of business and organisational skills not hitherto associated with general practice management.

General practitioners in the 1990s have moved to the centre of healthcare management, and practice management is now one of the fastest growing occupations in the NHS.

Crucial to the practice manager's role is the management of staff. For most enterprises – general practice is no exception – human effort more than anything else will make the difference between success and failure. This book brings together a series of articles written since 1990 on (mainly) staff management issues. Originally published in *Pulse*, *Financial Pulse*, the *BMJ*, *Medeconomics*, *Practice Manager*, and *Dentist* these articles are by no means a comprehensive (or necessarily original) examination of management issues. The topics covered represent those most often reported by practice managers and GPs as problem issues. Wherever possible I have incorporated checklists for action, which I hope will help busy readers to identify appropriate courses of action and provide a practical framework for tackling common managerial problems. Inevitably, certain subjects have required consideration of the surrounding legal framework. For a more detailed analysis of some of the legal issues, readers are advised to read *Employing Staff* by Norman Ellis (BMJ Publishing Group).

I gratefully acknowledge the help in compiling this book given to me by the staff in the BMA's north west office. I also thank the editors of those publications listed above for their kind permission to reprint (and in some cases update and modify) the original articles used.

PETER FORSTER
May 1995

1 Planning for new staff

The decision to appoint a new member of staff, or replace someone who has left, is one of the most crucial any practice will ever take. Getting the decision right however is not just a matter of being a good judge of character.

Demographic changes in the 1990s mean that GPs, in common with other employers, will experience difficulties in recruiting the right staff to fill practice vacancies. But this isn't the only reason that doctors should give careful consideration to their recruitment procedures. Employment problems later on – including disputes and conflicts with staff – can often be traced to poorly thought out recruitment and selection procedures. Moreover the recruitment of staff is an expensive business (especially when practices look for more sophisticated recruitment methods to help them select the right person). Management consultants have not been slow to recognise general practice in the 1990s as a new market for their often costly recruitment and selection services.

Getting the recruitment process wrong means not only unnecessary costs but can also result in poor staff performance, unnecessary training, higher absenteeism and turnover, and lower staff morale. The actual costs of selecting the wrong person for a job may be difficult to calculate but would include:

- Advertising,
- Time and resources spent recruiting,
- Travelling and other interview expenses,
- Salary and other benefits,
- National insurance contributions,

- Additional overheads,
- Training or induction costs,
- Opportunity costs (that is, the income the practice might have derived if the new employee had lived up to expectations),
- Costs and time finding a replacement.

To avoid unnecessary costs and potential employment problems later on, a practice should draw up a simple routine to follow each time a vacancy occurs. This should cover the following:

- Analysing and describing the job to be undertaken,
- Describing the ideal person to do the job,
- Drawing up a job advertisement.

Analysing and describing the job

When someone leaves a practice the tendency is always to recruit a replacement automatically. In every case, however, the first step should be to ask whether the practice needs to recruit a new employee. Alternatively, can the practice get along without replacing the person who is leaving? Could existing staff be trained to perform new tasks? If a vacancy needs to be filled then spending time at the outset assessing fully the job description will be worthwhile. This will result in a candidate who is better matched to the needs of the practice.

Finding the best person to fill a vacancy depends on finding an applicant who:

- Possesses the appropriate level of skill and qualifications;
- Can identify with the objectives, values, and aims of the practice;
- Sees themselves as making a positive and effective contribution to achieving these aims.

Analysing a job is a process of collecting information about the job and assessing it in terms of its context in the practice and the tasks and responsibilities involved. Many practices ignore the analysis stage and go straight to producing a job description. Job analysis should, however, be viewed as a foundation stone of successful staff selection. There are various ways in which the process can be undertaken:

- Interviewing existing staff about the nature of the work.
- Compiling a checklist or questionnaire to help identify the tasks and activities involved.
- Observing the work that goes on in the practice.
- Keeping a log – asking staff to keep a diary sheet to record their activities for later analysis.

Careful thought should be given to the questions that need to be asked to gather relevant information to assist in the job analysis. A checklist will help this task (see box 1).

Box 1 – Job analysis – checklist

Is there a vacancy in the practice?

- Has someone left?
- Are there new tasks to be done?
- Has the volume of the work increased or decreased?

Does the vacancy have to be filled?

- Can the practice get along without a replacement?
- Can existing staff be retrained or redeployed?
- Can the post be converted to a part time one?

Has the job changed, so requiring different skills or qualities?

How do I decide what work needs doing?

- Check existing job description
- Discuss with practice manager and other members of staff
- Observe staff doing the work
- Consider how to achieve important objectives that are not being achieved at present

What is the purpose of the job?

- What will be done?
- What will result from it?
- When will it be done?
- Where will it be done?
- How will it be done?
- What standards of performance are required?

Box 1 continued

What responsibilities does the jobholder have for:

- Subordinates?
- Money?
- Practice equipment?
- Confidential information?
- Deciding on working methods and practice?
- Deciding objectives and targets?

What working relationships (formal and informal) will the jobholder have with:

- Partners?
- Practice manager?
- Other practice staff?
- Family health services authority (FHSA)?
- District health authority (DHA)?
- Others?

What will be the job's:

- Pay (and bonuses)?
- Working conditions?
- Most challenging or attractive features?
- Most difficult (or unpleasant) aspects?

Writing a job description

Most people associate job descriptions with the recruitment and selection process, but having clear, concise, and up to date job descriptions can bring other benefits to the practice as well as to the individual employee (see box 2).

When recruiting staff GPs often reach for an existing job description (usually out of date). Instead, the information gathered during the analysis stage should be used to draw up a new job description. Before putting pen to paper ask the following questions:

Box 2 – Benefits of a job description

Benefits for the practice

- Defines individual tasks and duties as well as setting standards expected of the jobholder

- Provides the basis for reviewing individual performance, which can be used in staff appraisal schemes

- Helps justify the practice salary structure and can be used for upgrading or promotion purposes

- Identifies the training and learning needs of staff

- Helps in recruiting and selecting staff

- Gives support in dealing with disciplinary or grievance matters, dismissals, and industrial tribunal proceedings

- May provide a defence in proceedings under employment legislation (see separate box)

Benefits for the jobholder

- Sets out what is expected and the standards by which jobholder will be judged

- Provides an opportunity to take part in setting standards

- Helps to resolve job related problems

- Do we need to fill the job at all?
- Has the job changed, so requiring different qualities or skills?
- Even if the job has not changed, are there any extra qualities or skills we should look for in a new candidate?

The basis of writing a job description include the following:

Keep it simple – Avoid jargon, repetition, and complexity. The same format and style should be used throughout. Statements of skills, aptitude, and knowledge required should be specifically related to the needs of the job.

Do not exaggerate – Job descriptions often provide an opportunity for empire builders. This should be avoided. The description should be a factual and realistic statement of responsibilities. Statements of length and type of experience should be restricted to what is necessary for effective job performance.

5

Box 3 – Employment law and job description

1 Under the race relations and sex discrimination acts an employer may be required to justify shortlisting procedures, or the way in which an interview is conducted, or the criteria used for selection or promotion. The best way to do this is by systematic evidence derived from job descriptions.

2 Proposals set out in the Disability Discrimination Bill 1995 will have a major impact on employment practices. When the legislation comes into force disabled workers will be protected against discrimination by an employer from recruitment through to dismissal; although at present it is proposed that organisations with fewer than 20 employees will be exempt.

3 Under the Equal Pay Act, 1970 (as amended in 1983) employees are entitled to claim equal pay for work of equal value. Pressure is increasing on employers to adopt a more systematic and robust approach to job analysis and job descriptions, and to justify pay and grading structures so as to ensure that there is no discriminatory bias in the system.

Make sure job descriptions do not overlap – The job description should distinguish the job from every other job in the practice. Avoid duplication of responsibilities and duties.

Do not confuse job descriptions with person specification – The job description describes the job to be done, the person specification describes the ideal person to do the job. The essence of successful recruitment is to match the job (that is, the job description) with the profile of the ideal person (that is, the person specification).

Avoid discrimination – Criteria covering personal qualities should be directly related to the job and applied equally to all groups regardless of age, sex, race, creed, or disability (see box 3).

Structuring a job description

When possible a standard format and style should be adopted. A job description should cover the following topics:

Job title – This should be clear, understandable, and a realistic description of the job.

Position in the practice – In relation to other jobs – that is, which jobs are more senior and how many staff the jobholder supervises.

Principal purpose of the job – This should be a point of focus for the rest of the job description and encapsulate the main purpose of the job. A few brief sentences should do, but these must not be too complex or too bland.

Main duties and tasks – Here the job is broken down into its component parts. These should always relate to the principal purpose of the job in terms of importance (extremely important, important, or unimportant) and the amount of time spent performing them (for example, considerable, moderate, or very little).

Decision making and contacts – This should cover the amount of supervision the job has as well as the number of jobs supervised, the amount of discretion allowed, and the type of equipment or

---

Box 4 – Sample job description for practice manager

Job title: Practice Manager

Position in the practice

1 Responsible to Drs X, Y, and Z.
2 Supervision of three reception staff, two secretaries, one computer programmer, and one cleaner.

Principal purpose

To plan, organise, and manage all non-clinical aspects of the practice and to assist with the planning of future activities and developments so as to ensure that the highest standard of primary health is provided to patients.

Objectives

1 To plan, organise, and manage the practice reception area, appointment system, record filing, repeat prescribing arrangements, age/sex register, and GP diaires.
2 To manage all aspects of practice staffing including recruitment, selection, and retention of staff; to support, motivate, and develop the practice team.
3 To assist clinicians in assessing the healthcare needs and expectations of the practice population.
4 To ensure that adequate and effective financial procedures and systems are in place and to advise partners on all aspects of practice finance.
5 To act as a communication link between all members of the practice team to make sure resources are allocated so as to allow practice members to carry out their roles effectively.

7

Box 4 continued

6 To assist the partners in carrying out clinical audit.

7 To effect the optimum allocation of practice resources (time, money, staffing, and skill mix), and to manage the human resource function of the practice.

8 To ensure the maintenance and security of all practice premises and capital equipment.

9 To monitor, review, and maintain all aspects of the practice health and safety procedures, and to ensure that all staff are trained and made aware of health and safety legislation, regulations, and procedures.

10 To promote the interests and the nature of the practice at all times, and to ensure that an effective system of handling complaints is maintained.

11 To liaise with all outside agencies including the FHSA, NHS trusts, other healthcare providers, LMC, and deputising services.

Knowledge and experience required

The practice manager must possess leadership and communication skills combined with the ability to deal with issues with tact, diplomacy, and confidentiality.

In addition, good business and planning skills are required to ensure that the practice runs in the most efficient and effective manner. Management in a changing environment requires creativity and the qualities of adaptability and innovation are needed to develop the practice. In addition the practice manager must possess appropriate interpersonal skills and knowledge of all aspects of employment and staff management. It is also essential to have a sound knowledge of all aspects of relevant legislation, NHS practices and procedures, regulations, and FHSA requirements.

Conditions of service

Location: The practice manager is based at Yew Tree Health Centre but also has responsibility for the branch surgery at 25 Lily Terrace, Toytown.

Hours: normally 37½ Monday to Friday, but occasionally the job holder will be required to work in excess of this, after consultation with the partners.

Salary: £20 000 plus per annum
Salary review: annually on 1 April
Pension: Staff Care
Holiday: 5 weeks a year
Sick leave: As per schedule set out in the staff handbook

capital items used in performing the job. Information should also be given about the people the job holder comes into contact with, in what way, how often, and for what reasons.

Physical environment – This describes the physical conditions the work is to be done in, hours of work, any health hazards, etc.

Conditions of employment

Conditions of employment should cover all matters relating to salary, salary review, sickness absence, notice, holidays, etc. (Box 4 gives an example of a job description done in this style.)

When to write a job description

Ideally, a job description should already be written and completed before a person takes up the job. For existing staff, job descriptions should be written as soon as practicable and should always involve the staff concerned. In any event, job descriptions should always be reviewed regularly and updated.

Box 5 – Checklist for preparing personnel specification

	Essential	Desirable
1 Education	.....	.....
2 Qualifications	.....	.....
3 Experience	.....	.....
4 Innate ability (for example, mental agility)		
5 Specific ability and skills	.....	.....
6 Social skills	.....	.....
7 Personality	.....	.....
8 Physical makeup	.....	.....
9 Personal circumstances	.....	.....
10 Emotional adjustment (for example, coping with stress)		

Starting and maintaining an effective system of job descriptions is not easy and requires much effort and a disciplined approach.

Describing the best person to do the job

The profile of the best person suited to do a job is called a person specification. Information about the kind of person most suited to the job will emerge during the job analysis stage. Write out a list of characteristics you will be looking for in applicants. For example you might require a person with good reception and interpersonal skills, certain qualifications (such as an AMSPAR certificate), experience of operating a word processor or personal computer, experience in basic accounting methods, willingness to work overtime, etc. You should prepare a checklist indicating what would be the essential minimum, as well as the desirable ideals, from potential candidates (see box 5).

In compiling a person specification (as well as a job description) consider:

- Statement of skills, aptitude, and knowledge should be specifically related to the needs of the job
- Statements of length and type of experience should be restricted to what is necessary for effective job performance
- Potential training to help candidates achieve satisfactory job performance should be identified
- Educational and training requirements should not exceed the minimum requirements for satisfactory performance of the job
- Criteria covering personal qualities should be directly related to the job and applied equally to all groups regardless of age, sex, race, creed, or disability.

The essence of successful selection is to match the job (described in the job description) with the profile of the ideal person (described in the person specification). This process allows the practice to examine systematically the job and the characteristics it will be seeking from the ideal candidate.

Finding the right person – drawing up a job advertisement

Having described the job and the ideal person to fill it, the next stage is to find suitable applicants. Before placing an advertisement you should give consideration to other (cheaper) options:

Box 6 – Any job advertisement should include the following details:

The practice

- Information about the practice (such as whether it is fundholding)
- Number of patients
- Location
- Any branch surgeries

The job (based on job description)

- Nature and content of the job
- Duties and responsibilities
- Reason for vacancy (is it a new job?)
- Distinguishing features of the job

The applicant (based on the person specification)

- Distinguish between what is essential and what is desirable
- Include educational or other qualifications required
- Level and type of experience needed
- Type of personality
- Don't demand qualifications for which you are prepared to train people

Salary and benefits

- Minimum salary
- Performance supplement
- Pension arrangements
- Luncheon vouchers, etc
- Relocation assistance, if any

How to apply

- Application to whom
- Written applications, CVs, or application form
- Telephone number for informal discussion
- Further information (such as job description and job pack) from whom
- Closing date

- Are there suitable internal candidates?
- Could members of the practice staff recommend suitable candidates (from among friends and families)?
- What about patients? Note that consideration should always be given to possible conflicts that may arise from employing patients. What if, later, they can't work because of ill health? What if they have access to records on members of their own family?
- Do you still have details of unsuccessful applicants from previous practice vacancies?
- Have you checked job centres?
- Have you contacted local colleges that run practice staff, NHS, or management courses?
- Have you tried employment and selection agencies?

HAIGTOWN MEDICAL CENTRE

BUSINESS MANAGER c £25 000

— an exciting and innovative development in general practice

We are a six doctor fundholding practice with over 9000 patients, situated in one of the most scenic locations in the Central Highlands of Scotland.

Operating from new purpose built premises in the centre of Haigtown, we are fully computerised and now wish to recruit a Business Manager to manage the fund, negotiate contracts with provider units, and implement a strategic plan.

Candidates should possess leadership and communication skills as well as a thorough knowledge of computerised records system. Although not essential, experience of NHS management or general practice, or both, would be a definite advantage.

We are looking for an exceptional manager with appropriate professional qualifications in business management and accountancy as well as considerable experience of staff management, budgetary control systems, business planning and data collection.

Most important of all, you will be committed to maintaining an effective and responsive service to patient care of the highest standard.

Salary is negotiable but is expected to be at least £25 000 per annum.

For an informal discussion contact Dr Bloggs on 01932 662415. A job description can be obtained by writing to Haigtown Medical Centre, Haigtown, Scotland.

Written applications together with a CV

Haigtown Medical Centre operates a no smoking policy

Figures 1.1 – 1.4: Examples of job advertisements for practice posts

PRACTICE MANAGER

We are a busy five partner practice in the centre of Toytown with over 9000 patients. The practice is intending going fundholding in the next 12 months.

We are looking for an enthusiastic and innovative manager to join us at a time of considerable change. The job entails managing over 10 staff, including 2 practice nurses, 4 receptionists, 2 secretaries, and a computer programmer. The practice is fully computerised.

We welcome applicants with relevant qualifications and experience from a range of professional backgrounds. Essential requirements include proven managerial and leadership skills and experience of staff management and developing and maintaining an efficient administrative and computerised information system.

A knowledge of NHS or general practice, or both, is not essential but would be a distinct advantage.

Salary in the range of £23 000 to £25 000
Benefits include luncheon vouchers, staff pension, and performance related pay

For an informal discussion about the post telephone Dr Todd on 01241 873254
Written applications together with CV

Figure 1.2

If a decision has been made to advertise for a candidate, careful consideration should be given to (a) drawing up the job advertisement and (b) where it is placed.

Drawing up the job advertisement

The aim of the job advert is to (a) attract the right applicant, (b) deter the wrong people, and (c) create a good image.

Advertisements must not discriminate on the grounds of sex or race, except in specific circumstances as detailed under the relevant sections of the race relations or sex discrimination acts. Under the Disability Discrimination Bill 1995, currently before parliament, it will also be unlawful to discriminate on the grounds of disability. It is also undesirable to set arbitrary age limits in job advertisements (see chapter 28 on age discrimination). Figures 1.1 - 1.4 give sample job advertisements for practice posts.

PRACTICE SECRETARY

We are looking for an experienced and enthusiastic secretary to join our busy 5 partner practice in Toytown.

In addition to your secretarial skills, including 60 wpm typing, plus audio and WP experience, you will probably have some experience of the NHS and of general practice. Reporting to the practice manager, your duties will include directing incoming communications, liaison with patients, partners and the FHSA, and occasionally reception duties.

Attractive salary plus luncheon vouchers

Please send for an application form to

Mrs S Smith
Practice Manager
Toytown Health centre
Toytown

Figure 1.3

Telephone calls waiting, patients in the reception, and an emergency .... could you cope? If so we're waiting to hear from you.

RECEPTIONIST (part time)

We're looking for a cheerful receptionist to work 16 hours a week in a busy, but friendly, general practice.

The job entails handling all incoming calls, greeting patients and visitors, and informing staff and doctors of their arrival. Occasionally you will need to deal with complaints.

You will need a good telephone manner, a smart appearance, and the ability to remain calm and confident under pressure. Previous experience in a busy GP surgery together with switchboard skills would be desirable.

Please contact Mrs Brigss, Practice Manager for further details on 01 328 9211 or write to her at The Lodge, Meadowbank, Lenchester.

THE PRACTICE HAS A NO SMOKING POLICY

Figure 1.4

Placing an advertisement

Where an advertisement is placed will depend on who the practice wants to reach. Local papers are probably the best for receptionists and clerical jobs. For nursing or management posts, health service journals would be appropriate (for example, *Nursing Times, Health Service Journal, Practice Manager, Pulse,* etc). For senior posts, increasing numbers of practices are using national newspapers – including the *Independent*, which claims to have the highest level of NHS readers.

Following the process outlined in this chapter allows the practice to examine systematically a job and the characteristics it will be seeking from the ideal candidate. Choosing and finding the right person for a job leads to gains all round for the practice. The wrong choice can result in unnecessary expense and wasted time as well as considerable stress, anxiety, and disruption to the practice.

Induction programme for new staff

The proper induction of new staff is a vital part of any practice's recruitment procedures. Studies of staff turnover often show that new starters leave after only a few weeks in a job. This is called the "induction crisis". An induction programme gives a practice the opportunity to help new staff to understand what is going on and to help them fit into a new and unfamiliar environment quickly and without fuss. There is, however, more to it than just learning what work is required. The sooner you can help new staff tune in to the goals and expectations of the practice – and how members of the practice team relate to one another – the sooner they will become effective team members.

There are many other aspects of the practice about which a new recruit will require information. It is often helpful to prepare an induction checklist, but care should be taken not to give a new member of staff too much information at one time. A practice checklist might include the following:

- Written statement of main terms and conditions of service
- Probationary period
- Job title and description of duties
- Holiday arrangements
- Hours of work
- Notice period

- Sick pay arrangements
- Pension arrangements.

In addition to this type of information, which deals with the terms and conditions of employment, it would also be helpful to include the following items in a checklist:

- The structure of general medical services
- History of the practice
- Role of the family health services authority (FHSA), local medical committee (LMC), General Medical Services Committee (GMSC), British Medical Association (BMA)
- Role of purchasers and providers
- General information about patients
- Practice finance
- Structure of the practice and the services provided
- Current problems and concerns
- Rules and expectations
- Unwritten rules
- Confidentiality
- Handling complaints
- Staff rights and facilities.

In planning an induction programme for new staff, the practice manager should decide on how long the programme will last, how it will be monitored, and who should organise and carry it out. It might be desirable to provide new members of staff with some kind of printed reminder of some of the main points raised in the induction programme and an indication of where to go for further information. A practice "staff handbook" (see chapter 9) can be a useful aid and reference source during the induction period. In most cases it would be advisable to send a copy out in advance of a new recruit starting.

The following points should be remembered in an induction programme:

- Impressions gained by new staff can influence their perceptions of the practice for many years to come.
- Starting a new job is often associated with new lifestyles, unfamiliar travel and work routines, new relationships, and possibly a change of home. These factors contribute to a high level of anxiety, and the role of an effective induction

programme is to help minimise this anxiety and help new starters feel welcome at a new place of work.

• Do not make an induction programme too intense. New recruits can only take in a limited amount of information at any one time.

Further reading

Induction of New Employees. Advisory, Conciliatory and Arbitration Service (ACAS) advisory booklet No 7.

2 A word about references

The question of references will arise either when the practice is planning to recruit staff or when a former or departing employee applies for another job and the practice receives a request from a prospective employer.

Recruiting staff – taking up references

References are used by most employers. They have long been seen as a backstop – almost a formality – once a final decision to appoint has been made. They are used to: (a) verify information given by the candidate during the interview and contained in the application form or CV; (b) Give additional information or impressions of the candidate.

Taking up references can take various forms. A recent survey of

Type of approach	Used by % of employers
Telephone reference	6
Write to referee	30
Send report form	38
Telephone and send form	7
Write and send form	5
Telephone then write	5
Various	7

employers identified the types of approach and how much each was used (see box, page 18).

Despite their popularity among employers, references have a very poor reliability and validity record and are a very poor predictor of job performance. For these reasons practices should treat references from former employers with a healthy degree of scepticism. If references are to be used always get more than one for each applicant.

The application form at the time of interview should clearly state that the practice will not approach current or previous employers without the candidate's prior permission. Information obtained from a reference must be treated as confidential. It should be made clear, however, that the practice will be required to release references if information is required by a statutory agency investigating a complaint of discrimination. The practice

---

Private and Confidential

Dear Sir/Madam

Mr J Bloggs

The above named person has recently applied for a position with this practice and has given your name as a referee. We understand that he/she was previously employed by you as follows:

Employed by you from:
                to:

The applicant has applied for the post of practice manager and we would appreciate it if you would kindly answer the questions on the attached form concerning the applicant's suitability for this post. Any information you give will be treated in the strictest confidence and without any liability on your part.

A stamped addressed envelope is also enclosed for your convenience.

Thank you for your assistance in this matter.

Yours faithfully

For and on behalf of
Smith and Jones Partners

Encs

Figure 2.1 Request for a reference

Confidential

Mr J Bloggs

1. Are the details given in our covering letter correct? If not please state the correct period of employment and/or position held in your organisation.

. . . .

. . . .

2. Did you find the applicant honest and capable? Please give details of any assessment or opinion you may have on these matters.

. . . .

. . . .

3. Was the applicant   a) punctual?
                            b) capable?
                            c) reliable?
                            d) able to get on well with others?

4. Was the applicant able to work well under pressure?

. . . .

. . . .

5. Was the applicant able to work without supervision?

. . . .

. . . .

6. What was the applicant's absence record? Please give details of periods of absence.

. . . .

. . . .

7. Did the applicant ever receive any disciplinary warnings during the course of their employment? If so what were they for?

. . . .

. . . .

8. Why did the applicant leave your employment?

. . . .

. . . .

9. Would you re-employ the applicant?   YES ☐ (tick)
                                                 NO ☐ (tick)

10. Do you know any reason why we should not employ this
    person?

    . . . .

    . . . .

    Additional information

    . . . .

    . . . .

    . . . .

    . . . .

    Signature . . . .   Date . . . .

    For and on behalf of
    Smith Jones & Partners

Figure 2.2 Reference reply form

should be clear about the method to be used in approaching the
referee and should provide information about the job and ask
direct questions that will help identify the applicant's suitability
for the job. Figures 2.1 and 2.2 are models of a request letter and
form asking for a reference.

Giving references

Giving as well as taking up references is an important part of
the employment process. A practice is under no legal obligation to
give a reference unless it has agreed to do so in a contract of
employment or as part of a termination agreement. Failure to do
so, however, may cause hardship. Unless it is possible to convince
an enquirer that it is the practice policy never to give references, a
refusal may lead to the assumption that the individual left under
some sort of cloud.

Giving a reference is not without legal risk, although in practice
the risk is minimal. If a reference is given a practice should ensure
that it is not defamatory and that it is accurate. Misleading or
defamatory references have given grounds for action for
misrepresentation or negligence.

21

Defamation

If a reference contains a false or unprovable statement and it damages the reputation of the individual then an action for damages might result (a defence might be "qualified privilege").

Deceit or negligent misrepresentation

A practice writing a reference may have a legal liability to the new employers. Giving a glowing reference which is untrue and which is relied on by new employers to their detriment could lead to an action based on deceit or negligent misrepresentation. A sensible precaution might be to write "without legal responsibility" at the top of any reference.

Neutral references

If GPs feel obliged to respond to a request for a reference they could try the "estate agent approach" (sometimes called the neutral reference). This entails conveying the truth about someone without actually saying anything detrimental. It is similar to estate agents' art of composing descriptions of properties for sale.

Inaccurate references

Employees who are given inaccurate references based on information stored on a computer may be entitled to bring an action under the Data Protection Act, 1984. This would be for compensation for any loss suffered as a result. They should also be able to have the data corrected or if necessary erased.

3 Mastering interview techniques

Interviewing is one of those activities that people always seem to think they are good at – driving a car is another! Managers often assume their experience and managerial skills will easily enable them to get the measure of someone during an interview. Evidence, however, suggests that lots of mistakes can be made: such as asking the wrong questions, failing to separate out the important information from the unimportant: making one's mind up about an individual on the basis of initial appearances rather than deciding on the basis of the facts.

Interviewing is a skill that involves a lot more than meeting someone, having a chat, and making up your mind what you think of them. Ill prepared or poorly conducted interviews can be costly to a practice in terms of money, time, poor recruitment, and staff morale.

Purposes of interviews

Mention interviews, and most people think of recruitment. But there is a wide range of other work contexts where interviewing is essential.

Performance appraisal—where staff and managers discuss standards of performance, strengths, and weaknesses with a view to developing an employee's full potential.

Grievance handling—handling disputes and conflicts involving individual staff members.

Disciplinary procedures—to effect a change in an employee's work performance or behaviour, or both.

Counselling interview—aimed at helping an employee to identify the causes of a problem and to get a new perspective on a problem that may be influencing their work performance.

Exit interview—to gain information about an employee's decision to resign, either to persuade them to stay or to assess replacement requirements to prevent future resignations.

Selection and recruitment—an opportunity to identify potential candidates for jobs and to allow candidates to find out about the job and the practice.

All interviews involve a two way flow of information; it is usually personal in the sense that the interviewee is at the centre of the discussion. The aim is usually to enable both interviewer and interviewee to decide on the most effective future course of action.

Many pitfalls face managers when conducting an interview. The more common problems include:

- Lack of clarity about the objectives of the interview;
- Failure to work out which topics are likely to elicit the most useful information;
- Failure to structure the interview properly;
- Failure to provide the right physical setting;
- Failure to ask the right questions and in the right way;
- Talking too much;
- Not listening;
- Jumping to conclusions;
- Failure to probe, especially in what look like areas of weakness;
- Low recall of information;
- Bias or prejudice in evaluation;
- A tendency to try and assess the interviewee as a whole rather than building up a picture systematically;
- Concentration on personality traits rather than results and behaviour;
- Lack of effective follow up.

Interviews are not always easy and can at times be extremely stressful. If a manager has done her or his homework, however, there is much more chance of the interview achieving its objectives.

Interviewing strategy

There is no "right" way to conduct an interview; it always depends on a manager's particular style and personality. As part

A simple interview plan

Interview stage	Objectives	Activities
Beginning	Put candidate at ease Develop rapport Set the scene	Greet candidate by name Introduce self Neutral chat Agree interview purpose Outline how purpose will be achieved
Middle	Collect and give information Maintain rapport	Ask questions within a structure Listen Observe Answer questions
End	Close interview Confirm future action	Summarise interview Check candidate has no more questions Say what happens next

of the preparation for an interview, an interviewer needs to devise the appropriate strategy to suit the situation and his or her own temperament. Common approaches to interview include:

"Tell me all about it" approach: this is aimed at putting interviewees at their ease. At every stage the interviewer is open, friendly, and shows a genuine interest in the interviewee.

"You can tell me, it will go no further" approach: again, aimed at putting interviewees at their ease. This approach allows people to unburden themselves, without the fear of the matter going further. This is a useful approach in a counselling situation, although employees may be reluctant to bare their souls in a one to one interview with their manager.

Joint problem solving approach: this is a useful approach in a disciplinary or grievance situation. It usually involves the manager and employee agreeing on a joint approach to solving a problem and a joint plan of action for the future. This approach inevitably results in lots of "we" solutions and, it is hoped, ensures full commitment on the part of the employee to resolving the problem.

Tell and sell approach: this approach involves the interviewer persuading the interviewee towards a particular point of view, or "selling" the interviewee a solution advocated by the interviewer.

25

This strategy can be used to some effect in performance appraisal and grievance interviews, but may prove disastrous in other contexts. For example, in selection interviewing where an applicant is persuaded (on the basis of a brief conversation) to take a job, without full consideration being given to the suitability of either the job or the candidate.

"Stress" strategy: this is the opposite of the "tell me all about it" tactic and relies on the assumption that an interviewee will reveal more about themselves when under pressure. The technique – like the Spanish inquisition – involves challenging the interviewee's beliefs, ridiculing their opinions and questioning their achievements. Some companies use this approach in selecting staff to try to identify individuals with higher levels of assertiveness and tolerance. Of course, such an approach has to be skilfully handled and would be inappropriate in a disciplinary or grievance handling context.

"Mr Nasty and Mr Nice" approach: using this approach, one interviewer pressurises the interviewee by using "stress" tactics then leaves the interview in the hands of "Mr Nice" who turns a sympathetic ear and may apologise for the approach of his colleague. At this point the interviewee, in his or her relief, supposedly tells all.

Conducting an interview

In any interviewing situation it is essential to have an interviewing plan (see box). Next, you need to decide on what questions to ask, how to ask them and how to conduct the interview. With most interviews it will be possible to draw up a checklist of points to be explored. In asking questions the following points should be borne in mind:
- Always ask questions in a logical sequence (for instance chronologically)
- If possible, link each new question to the last reply
- Avoid multiple questions (for example, How long were you at your last practice, did you enjoy it, and why did you leave?)
- Steer clear of jargon. (Unless someone has previous experience of the NHS the question: "How would you ensure that the FP 73s got off to the FHSA on time" would not mean much to the interviewee.)

- Ask open questions ("What do you enjoy most about your current job?").
- Summarise and check how far you have got.
- Ask probing questions to check important facts and statements ("Why do you say that?").
- Encourage the interviewee to talk and link questions ("What happened next?").
- Avoid yes/no questions (you always get the same answer to the question "Do you get on well with people?").
- Don't ask leading questions. (Leading questions give the answer the interviewer is looking for in asking the question. The interviewee will usually oblige by giving the answer he knows you are looking for.)
- Don't criticise the interviewee (unless using a "stress" strategy).
- Give interviewees time to think about their answers. Never think that you must rush in with a supplementary question just because there is a pause in the conversation.
- Don't be afraid of silence; often it is the best way of getting people talking.
- Always look interested.
- Avoid extreme mannerisms, verbal or physical (eg playing with a pen or excessive use of "umms" and "errs" and overused phrases such as "at this moment in time").
- Listen, listen, and listen.
- Don't jump to conclusions by putting words into the interviewee's mouth: allow them to finish and to develop their answers fully.
- Avoid prejudice and bias. Your judgment of the interview should be based on the facts and not on your biases.

Physical arrangements

You need to decide who is to participate in the interview (for example, one or more of the partners and/or the practice manager). Is a briefing meeting required? Make sure the interviewee knows when and where the interview is to take place. Final preparations will include deciding who is to ask what questions, in what order, and who will take notes (particularly important in disciplinary interviews). Again a checklist is helpful (see box overleaf).

A checklist

- Will the interview location be available at the required time?
- Has the interviewee been notified of the time and place of the interview, the identity of the interviewer, and the likely duration of the interview?
- Have other interviewers, if any, been advised of the time and place of the interview and met to discuss their strategy and tactics?
- Has the receptionist been told who to expect, when, and where to direct them?
- Have arrangements been made not to interrupt the interview by telephone calls or personal visits?
- Has everyone had sufficient notice of the event?
- Have appropriate refreshments been arranged?
- If the interviewee has to travel to the interview, have arrangements been made to pay the appropriate expenses or allowances?
- If the interviewee has had to be absent from normal duties, have arrangements been made?
- Is action in hand to deal with the outcome of the interview?

Interviewing requires careful and detailed planning, and, like other management tasks, requires considerable skill. Skills in interviewing techniques are, of course, best developed by "doing" rather than by reading up the latest management texts.

4 Employing staff – make it legal

Good practice management policies will largely ensure that employee relations problems are resolved positively and without recourse to formal or legal proceedings. Nevertheless, it is important for practice managers to understand the increasingly complex legal framework they operate in. This framework is dealt with in detail in *Employing Staff* by Norman Ellis (BMJ Publishing Group). This chapter summarises the important legal issues surrounding the employment contract – forming the contract, varying a contract, and bringing a contract to an end. Chapter 5 deals with the topic of fixed term contracts.

What is a contract of employment?

An employment contract like any other contract is an agreement involving an offer and acceptance, supported by consideration (that is, wages) and an intention by both parties to be legally bound. A contract does not have to be in writing, it may simply involve a verbal agreement.

Many statutory rights become applicable when an employment contract is entered into, although several of these depend on length of employment (see box 1) as well as terms and conditions reached through collective agreement (such as pay rates reached through the General Whitley Council). The terms of a contract can also be ascertained by reference to other documents such as an

Box 1 – Employees have statutory rights to:

- Not be discriminated against on grounds of race
- Not be discriminated against on grounds of sex
- Equal pay for equal work, for work of equal value, or work rated as equivalent
- An itemised pay statement
- Maternity benefits
- Notice of termination of employment
- Payment in cash where existing employees have established a contractual right
- Guaranteed pay when laid off
- Redundancy pay
- A safe system of work
- Statutory sick pay
- Time off for public duties; for trade union activities, duties, and training; and to look for work if declared redundant after at least two years' service
- Belong or not belong to a trade union and to take part in trade union activities
- Protected employment rights when a business is transferred to a new employer
- Not be unfairly dismissed
- Written reasons for dismissal (on request)
- A written statement of the particulars of employment
- Protection against dismissal or unfavourable treatment for taking certain actions on health and safety grounds
- Protection against dismissal for asserting a statutory right
- Be able to apply to an industrial tribunal for a declaration that the terms in a collective agreement or works rules are discriminatory on the grounds of sex

offer of employment letter, a job description, and staff handbook. Where there is uncertainty or ambiguity, terms can be "implied" from custom and practice or from what a court or industrial tribunal consider were the intentions of the parties.

Box 2 – Written particulars of employment

A written statement must be given within two months of the employee's start date to all employees employed 8 hours a week for over 1 month.

Content and format – core information must be given in one single written statement called the Principal Statement. The items included are:

- Names of employer and employee

- Date employment began

- Date continuous employment began

- Job title or brief description of job

- Pay, pay scale, or method of calculating pay, and payment interval

- Place of work or the required or permitted places of work along with the employer's address

- Hours of work including any terms and conditions relating to normal hours

- Holiday entitlement, including public holidays and holiday pay

The following additional information must be given, either in the same principal statement or in other instalments provided that all is given within 2 months, about:

- Terms and conditions for sickness, injury, and sick pay

- Pensions

- Notice periods

- Where the employment is not intended to be permanent, the expected length or the end date if fixed term

- Particulars of any collective agreements that directly affect the individual's terms and conditions

- Grievance procedures

- Disciplinary rules and procedures, including appeals procedures (this only applies in organisations where the number of employees employed directly or by an associate employer is 20 or more)

31

Box 2 continued

Reference documents – the written statement may refer the individual to other reference documents for the details of:

- Sickness, injury, and sick pay

- Pensions

- Discipline

- Applicable collective agreements and to the law or collective agreements for details on:

- Notice periods.

Changes to written particulars

- Any change must be notified to employees individually and in writing as early as possible and at the latest within 1 month

- The written notification may refer the employee to updated documents for details of items for which reference documents are allowed

Verbal contracts

A contract of employment may be entered into verbally – although defining its terms may be difficult. The Employment Protection (Consolidation) Act, 1978, as amended by the Trade Union Reform and Employment Rights Act, 1993, requires an employer within two months of the start of employment, to provide an employee (employed for over 1 month and working 8 or more hours a week) with a written statement setting out certain terms and conditions (see box 2). If an employer fails to provide such a statement an employee may apply to an industrial tribunal. The tribunal may specify the terms that ought to be included in the statement.

What are the benefits of having a written contract?

Many disputes over contracts, as well as unfair dismissal cases, concern either the lack of any written terms or their lack of clarity. As unwritten policies and procedures (often interpreted as custom and practice) can be used in legal proceedings, it is a good idea to have them documented in a way that the practice wants them interpreted, not the way an industrial tribunal may interpret them.

In any event, it is always good management practice to provide employees with all relevant employment documentation, such as contracts, job descriptions, staff handbook, etc.

Job advertisements

Generally a job advert does not give rise to any contractual obligations. If written terms are ambiguous or there are no written terms and conditions, however, an industrial tribunal or court may look at a job advert to interpret the contract. Care always has to be taken with job adverts, so as not to discriminate against applicants on grounds of race, ethnic origin, sex, or marital status. The Equal Opportunities Commission and the Commission for Racial Equality are empowered to bring proceedings in cases of alleged discriminatory adverts. Under the Disability Discrimination Bill 1995 disabled workers will be protected at all stages of the employment process against discrimination by an employer because of disability.

Ending a contract

An employer can lawfully end a contract by giving sufficient notice. The law requires an employer to give at least one week's notice, up to a maximum of 12 weeks, for each year of service. The exception to this is where an employee commits an act of gross misconduct (such as breach of confidentiality, theft, or violence) justifying summary dismissal, – that is, without notice. An employee can subject a decision to terminate the contract to a test of fairness before an industrial tribunal. This is where the law of unfair dismissal comes in. In most circumstances a case of unfair dismissal can only be brought by an employee who has been employed for two or more years. The exceptions to this are in cases of dismissal which are connected with racial or sexual discrimination, pregnancy, unfair selection for redundancy, or an employee's membership or non-membership of a trade union.

Many GPs hold the mistaken view that it is virtually impossible

---

Box 3—Fair reasons for dismissal

- The employee's *capability* to perform the job. (This may be for reasons such as ill health, poor performance, or lack of qualifications.)

- An employee's *conduct* such as persistent lateness or absenteeism, breaking practice rules, etc.

- *Redundancy* (but remember the law defines what redundancy is, and it cannot be used to get rid of someone. Also, when a redundancy arises selection must be fair and in accordance with any customary procedure (for example, based on the "last in first out" principle)).

- Where it would be *illegal* for someone to continue to work – for example, a taxi driver who loses his or her driving licence.

- "Some other substantial reason". This is a bit of a catch-all. In the past tribunals have justified dismissals under this heading for reasons such as an employee's refusal to go along with business reorganisation, difficulties with other employees (that is personality clashes), pressure from customers, the imprisonment of the employee, lying on an application form, and the persistent intermittent short term illness of an employee.

---

to dismiss a member of staff without being landed with a substantial award of compensation. The law, however, recognises several potentially fair reasons for dismissal (see box 3).

As well as being fair, a dismissal must also be carried out reasonably. This usually means following the rules of natural justice, which would involve: (a) informing the employee about any allegation, (b) undertaking a thorough investigation, (c) allowing for a fair and impartial disciplinary hearing, (d) allowing an employee to state his or her case and to be represented, (e) allowing an employee to appeal against any decision that results in disciplinary action.

Practices should have an up to date disciplinary procedure (see recommended reading). This should be drawn to the attention of all employees and be referred to in the contract.

Part time employees

On 3 March 1994 the House of Lords upheld a case brought by the Equal Opportunities Commission that the provisions of the Employment Protection (Consolidation) Act, 1978 on redundancy and unfair dismissal as regards part time employees working fewer than 8 or 16 hours a week were discriminatory and contrary to European Community law. Different qualifying rules for part time staff to acquire further statutory rights (for example, unfair dismissal and redundancy pay) were abolished from 6 February 1995. GPs should ensure that part time staff are treated in exactly the same way as full timers.

Varying a contract of employment

In recent years many GPs have had to consider making changes in the practice, which would result in having to amend or vary staff contracts – for example, changing working hours or working practices. It is important that changes are discussed and agreed where possible with the job holder, as imposing changes can be fraught with legal difficulties.

The basic legal position is that a contract can be changed lawfully only with the agreement of both sides. Unless a contract allows for changes, by having a flexibility clause (for example, "your normal hours will be . . . . but you may be required to work additional hours as are required"), then an employer is bound to obtain the employee's agreement before changing it. When changes are imposed and the employee works in accordance with the new terms without objection, then agreement may be "implied". When changes are imposed and employees carry on working under protest, however, they retain their right to sue for breach of contract. Alternatively they could resign in response to the imposed changes and claim constructive dismissal. An employer could instead terminate the existing contract lawfully and introduce a new one which incorporates modified terms. In such circumstances the employee could resign and claim unfair dismissal. In a significant judgement involving a case of constructive dismissal where an employee refused the offer of new contractual terms, the Court of Appeal said that the dismissal was nevertheless fair under the heading "some other substantial reason" because of the employer's "sound, good business reasons".

Seeking agreement is always the best course, but when GPs are faced with the need to vary a contract they should always seek expert advice.

As small employers, GPs should devote some time to employment issues. After all, staff are a practice's most valuable asset. Time and effort should be given to ensure that appropriate documents are drawn up. Employing people can, if handled badly, cost a GP time and money, not to mention the associated stress and anxiety.

5 Employment contracts – a fixed term option

Changing work patterns, the need for greater flexibility at the workplace, and the uncertainties created by market conditions in the NHS has resulted in the increased use of temporary and fixed term employment contracts. This has been particularly the case at senior management level in NHS trust hospitals. General practice has not been immune from these wider developments in the employment field. The vagaries of family health service authority (FHSA) funding and the need for more innovative approaches to the recruitment of staff have meant more and more practices looking at alternatives to the traditional (that is, no termination date) employment contract.

Contract law is complicated; in particular, the legal provisions relating to fixed term contracts and can pose problems for busy practice managers. Before contemplating using temporary or fixed term contracts, managers are advised to always seek expert advice and guidance.

What is a fixed term contract?

The use of fixed term contracts in general practice is increasingly being considered. There are, however, certain things to bear in mind when they are used. Practices should clearly understand at the outset the full implications of employing

Fixed term contract

Advantages

- It may be appropriate where uncertainty exists about the permanent need for a post, or the future availability of FHSA funding for the post

- They may be of value for short term projects as staff are employed for the duration of the project only

- Terminating the contract is easier because the practice can allow it to expire without renewing it

- A waiver clause in the contract will exclude unfair dismissal and redundancy claims thereby eliminating the possibility of lengthy and expensive tribunal proceedings

- There may well be a greater incentive for the employee to perform well to secure the renewal of the contract

Disadvantages

- Hiring a succession of employees might make it difficult to maintain continuity

- Commitment to the practice may be reduced

- Long term career development and motivation may be adversely affected

- Use of such contracts could affect the climate of employer and employee relations in the practice

- There could be pressure for enhanced pay or conditions of service to be applied in recompense for the contract being fixed term

- It may become difficult to attract candidates with the right experience because of the lack of long term job security

- It may be difficult and expensive to dismiss an employee fairly before the expiry of the contract

- Experienced staff with essential skills may be lost when the contract expires

staff on fixed term contracts, as these have advantages and disadvantages for both the practice and the employee (see box).

Fixed term contracts can take one of three main forms: (a) a contract with a specific termination date, (b) a contract discharged

Waiver clause

In accordance with Section 142 of the Employment Protection (Consolidation) Act 1978, I agree to waive my right to:
    (a) make a complaint of unfair dismissal★
    (b) a redundancy payment★
★delete where applicable

on the expiry of the contract on _____

I accept the appointment as _____

on the above terms and conditions and that it will come to an end on

_____

Signed: _____

Date: _____

Figure 5.1 Example of a waiver clause

by performance, or (c) a contract terminated on the occurrence or non-occurrence of a future event.

Specific termination date contract

This is the most common form of fixed term contract. Here a contract is for a fixed term and it is agreed at the outset that it will end on a specified date. The contract expires on that date without either side needing to give notice. However, either the practice or the employee may wish to end the contract before its expiry date. It would therefore be advisable to include notice provisions to allow the contract to be terminated by either party before it is due to end. Without such provision, if the practice terminates the contract prematurely it may be liable to a claim for damages for unpaid remuneration in respect of the rest of the contract.

To protect employees from being denied remedies against unfair dismissal by being repeatedly engaged on a series of fixed term contracts, employment protection legislation provides that the expiry without renewal of a fixed term contract constitutes a dismissal. An employee on a fixed term contract therefore has the same rights to claim compensation for unfair dismissal and redundancy pay as other dismissed employees. These rights are subject to the normal continuous service qualifying period of two years, and a dismissal may or may not be fair depending on the circumstances.

Unfair dismissal rights may, however be contracted away in certain circumstances. The law says that employees appointed for a single term of one year or more can be asked by their employers to agree in writing to waive their right to bring an unfair dismissal claim. This one year limit has remained despite the extension of the continuous service qualifying period granted for dismissal claims from the one year to two years. If the fixed term is for two years or more employees can also be asked to agree in writing to waive their right to bring a claim for a redundancy payment. Waivers will only be valid at the time the contract is due to come to an end. They will not be valid if the employer terminates the contract before that date. To continue to be effective, a waiver must be renewed if a fixed term contract is renewed, as the earlier waiver lapses. Waiver clauses will only be valid if they are in writing and agreed to by the employee before the contract expires. An example of a waiver clause can be seen in figure 5.1.

Contract to perform a specific task

A contract may be offered and accepted for the completion of a specific or "one-off" job or project and will automatically terminate once that task or project comes to an end. This kind of contract would only be suitable for a clearly recognisable "one-off" task and when no date is being used as the end point. No notice is required to terminate the contract when the job is finished – it is said to be "discharged by performance". There is no dismissal in law, and the employee cannot therefore put in a claim to an industrial tribunal for unfair dismissal or redundancy pay. When such a contract is used it would be advisable to include notice provisions, so that if necessary the contract can be terminated before the job is finished; this, however, will constitute a dismissal.

Contract terminable on the occurrence or non-occurrence of a future event

A variation on a contract to perform a specific task is a contract that will terminate on the occurrence or non-occurrence of a future event, such as discontinuation of family health service authority (FHSA) funding for a post. In a recent case an employee was offered and accepted a written contract which said:

> The appointment will last only as long as sufficient funds are provided either by the Manpower Services Commission or by other firms/sponsors to fund it.

When funding did cease and the contract was terminated the employer refused to make a redundancy payment on the basis that the contract was one to perform a specific task. The employer argued that the contract had been discharged by performance and therefore no dismissal had occurred. The Employment Appeal Tribunal agreed that no dismissal had taken place and therefore no redundancy payment needed to be made, but preferred the view that the contract was terminable by the occurrence or non-occurrence of a future event rather than the contract being for a specific task.

A contract terminable on the future happening or non-happening of an event will be recognised as such by the courts only if the event the contract depends on is beyond the control of both parties and when a clear causative link between the occurrence or non-occurrence of the event and the existence of the job can be established. This type of contract is relatively new and untested, so practices need to proceed cautiously if introducing one.

Appointing staff on temporary and fixed term contracts

When a practice wishes to appoint somebody on a temporary or fixed term contract, having considered the advantages and disadvantages of such contractual arrangements, they should make sure that in all cases the employee understands from the outset: (a) that the employment is temporary, (b) why it is temporary, (c) how long it is likely to last, (d) what event will bring it to an end, and (e) any special conditions of service relating to it.

In the case of a fixed term contract the employee should also understand (a) the date on which the contract will expire, and (b) the effective waiver clauses where they are inserted.

In all cases this information should be set out clearly in writing and in the letter of appointment and any written contract of employment or statement of particulars given. The offer should also be accepted, in writing, as being temporary on the conditions set out.

Terminating a fixed term contract

The fact that a contract is "fixed term" does not necessarily remove from the practice the legal obligation to follow the procedures that would accompany the termination of a permanent contract. Much will depend on the type of temporary employment contract that is used and whether it provides for termination by notice. As a general guide it is advisable to:

- Make sure the employee knows at the earliest opportunity when the contract is due to end;
- Consider carefully and at the earliest possible date whether the contract should be renewed and if so when;
- If the contract is not to be renewed, be clear about the reason for termination and start consultation as early as possible;
- Consider offering alternative employment, if appropriate, when the contract comes to an end.

6 The ideal practice manager

NHS reforms since 1990 have changed the face of general practice management. Moves from a hospital led service to one led by primary care, the creation of a managed but competitive internal healthcare market, and a performance based GP contract have all had far-reaching consequences for the traditional practice management function. In many cases this has led to a shake-out as GPs have come to realise that the traditional model of practice management no longer fits the bill. In others the manager's traditional role has been eclipsed by the appointment of fund or business managers – resulting in conflict in some cases.

Practice managers have always come in different shapes and sizes – from supervisor or general manager to administrator or senior receptionist. Unfortunately the role – long perceived to be outside mainstream NHS management – has suffered an image problem, or as some perceived it, the so called "Doris" factor. This image is no longer appropriate.

Practice management is one of the fastest growing occupations in the NHS, and today's general practice requires managers who are much more in the textbook manager mould. They should be able to:

- Manage themselves and others
- Demonstrate a clear understanding and appreciation of human resource management
- Demonstrate an understanding of leadership and the management of change

- Demonstrate the use of theoretical concepts in decision making and organisational change
- Identify their own leadership style and framework for adapting that style in general practice.

Combined with these features is the need for a range of business skills and experience, including:

- Health needs assessment
- Financial and budgeting management
- Business and strategic planning
- Marketing
- Contracting and negotiation
- Audit and quality management
- Public relations.

The recruitment of managers from business and industry (as well as from the ranks of NHS managers who have retired early or been made redundant) has increased greatly; doubtless they have been attracted by salaries approaching (and in some cases above) £30 000.

In 1993 the first national conference for practice managers was held under the auspices of the Institute of Health Services Management (IHSM), and in 1994 the Association of Health Care and Practice Administrators (AHCPA) changed its name to the Association of Managers in General Practice (AMGP) to identify more closely with the growing demands of the profession of practice management. Links have been established between the association, the Open University, and the Open Learning Foundation to enable practice managers to acquire formal management qualifications. The management education scheme by open learning (MESOL) gives practice managers access to the NHS's own management development programme. The association is also currently pioneering a version of management charter standards. So what should GPs now be looking for when recruiting a practice manager?

The management role

The traditional definitions of a practice manager's work are usually so broad as to be meaningless: "To make decisions," "Getting things done through people," "To control, direct, and motivate" and so on. In fact the role is less easily defined and less tidy than many management writers would have us believe. One way of looking at the management function is to define it in terms of constraints, choices, and demands.

Constraints are factors that limit managers' ability to do what they would like to do (for example, the attitudes and expectations of the partners, practice policies, legal requirements, staff shortages, lack of equipment, or lack of inherent skill and experience).

Choices entail deciding what work is to be done from a vast array of options (what work is done, when it is done, by whom, how it is done, what standards apply, etc).

The *demands* of the job dictate what a manager must do (for example, tasks dictated by partners, the FHSA, and practice targets or standards).

Another approach is to see the manager's role as a leader, administrator, and fixer. These roles can in turn be further subdivided (see box).

The mix of roles will vary from practice to practice, depending on its size, culture, and position but every management role has some of each.

The practice manager's roles

The leader (interpersonal role)

• Figurehead (that is, to represent the practice formally)

• Liaison officer (with peers and outsiders to swap information)

• Leader (to motivate staff)

The administrator (informational role)

• Monitor (to gather and store information)

• Disseminator (to pass on information)

• Spokesperson (to pass out information)

The fixer (decisional role)

• Entrepreneur (to initiate change)

• Disturbance handler (to take charge when the organisation is threatened)

• Resource allocator (to decide where and how resources will be deployed)

• Negotiator (to deal with outsiders whose consent and cooperation is required)

Manager as leader

The practice manager manages by influence and leadership (and not always by their "positional" authority). Leadership is about getting the job done by other people and involves qualities of imagination, courage, and sensitivity. The manager is responsible for getting tasks done and for the people performing them. A useful checklist of leadership qualities might include:

- Sharing with staff one's enthusiasm about what they are doing
- Allocating work in such a way as to promote the satisfaction and development of staff members as well as getting the job done
- Reminding all individual staff members about the purpose and importance of their work
- Communicating positive and negative feedback as appropriate
- Assisting staff to improve at their jobs and providing a challenge in the job
- Reviewing jobs with the aim of improving job satisfaction
- Involving staff and setting objectives, targets, or goals
- Involving staff members in decision making, and delegating when appropriate
- Explaining all decisions, and accepting any criticism as a basis for improvement
- Showing responsiveness to suggestions and grievances
- Ensuring that staff members who break important rules are not allowed to do so with impunity
- Monitoring progress and keeping practice staff informed
- Defending staff when work has been criticised
- Demonstrating to staff that you care about them as individuals and recognise that their work will be affected by what is happening in the rest of the lives.

Human resource role

The personnel or human resource management function – as we now call it – is a fundamental part of the practice manager's role. In general practice, as with most enterprises, human effort more than anything else makes the difference between success and failure. Practice success, and even survival in a managed but competitive NHS environment, will increasingly depend to a greater extent on the proper management and treatment of staff. Today's practice manager must show a clear understanding of the principles of good human resource management (see box).

The most important elements of human resource management

- Commitment (to promote teamwork, cooperation, and interest; and to create a climate in which all staff are motivated to meet the objectives of the practice)
- Communication (to act as the main link in communications between partners, staff, patients, the family health services authority (FHSA), purchasers, and providers)
- Performance (to ensure that staff performance is geared to the needs of the practice by maintaining proper performance and appraisal schemes)
- Recruitment and retention (to clarify needs and translate these into job descriptions, personnel specifications, and pay systems that will secure and retain the best staff)
- Training (to identify training needs of staff. To coordinate, evaluate, and (where necessary) conduct training)
- Employee relations (to maintain and develop good employee relations)
- Motivation (to motivate staff and encourage participation and decision making, and to foster a sense of responsibility and commitment to the practice)
- Delegation (to delegate duties and routine tasks to other members of the practice team in accordance with the skills and knowledge of each staff member)
- Decision making (to set priorities and keep staff informed of decisions)
- Discipline and grievance handling (to operate appropriate procedures and ensure fairness and reasonableness in all matters relating to discipline and grievance handling)

An NHS led by primary care can only be built on well managed practices. In such an environment the role of the practice manager is crucial. Today's practice managers must firmly identify themselves with the challenges faced by the practice on all levels – the drive to improve what is done today and the need to take on new roles and challenges tomorrow. Once seen as the bottom rung of the NHS management ladder, practice management has now come into its own.

7 The perfect receptionist

The stereotype of the practice receptionist as some kind of ogre, indifferent to the needs and anxieties of the patients and ensconced behind a bandit screen, still prevails in many people's minds.

Yet the demands of general practice in the 1990s demands a high degree of professionalism on the part of the receptionist; sensitive to patient needs, aware of the need to promote a positive image of the practice and equipped with the organisational skills needed in a busy working environment.

Projecting the right image

Can you remember the impression you received of the receptionist when you first visited a GP? Patients tend to judge the practice from the reception desk. First impressions are important. (Remember the adage you never get a second chance to create a good first impression.)

A good receptionist should be

- Polite
- Friendly but descreet
- Helpful
- Calm and patient
- Smart and well groomed
- Well informed about practice procedures
- Confident.

It is certainly not a job for a person who is shy or is subject to moody behaviour. In appearance the receptionist needs to be neat and smart. It is vitally important that a receptionist pays particular attention to personal appearance.

Good communications

The receptionist is a focal point of contact for patients, doctors, other practice staff, and other visitors to the practice. Communication skills are therefore important. All visitors to the practice should be treated with respect and courtesy. Receptionists should greet visitors with a smile and ascertain the nature of their visit. The aim should be to put visitors at ease and to listen carefully to what they have to say.

Personal qualities

Patients and visitors alike should be treated with respect and even though some may be anxious or even angry they should be dealt with patiently and tactfully. A receptionist has also to maintain confidentiality and be discreet and loyal to patients in the practice. This is not always easy, because a seemingly innocent (or careless!) remark may be more damaging than is first realised. Because the receptionist deals with so many people both inside and outside the practice, she may often hear rumours or gossip which she must tactfully try to discourage and certainly never repeat.

Education and experience

It is difficult to be prescriptive here, but, generally speaking, a good level of education and training is required. Although not always essential, previous experience of general practice and medical procedures would be desirable. As far as personal qualities are concerned, your person specification might include the following:

- A pleasant and cheerful personality;
- Ability to be able to relate to patients with empathy and understanding;
- Ability to work unsupervised with a high degree of accuracy;
- Discretion, loyalty, and tact;

Duties and responsibilities

- Ensure patient notes are checked and available for the GP
- Keep reception records
- Check that rooms are clean and tidy before surgery (including clean speculae, vaccines, and couch roll)
- Maintain a list of surgeries and clinics which are due to be held on any day
- Ensure all patients and visitors are treated courteously and appropriate details taken
- Deal with telephone and other enquiries as appropriate
- Arrange appointments in accordance with practice appointments procedure
- Ensure messages are passed on using the practice message sheets
- Arrange patient records according to practice procedures, eg. visits – brown book; messages – blue book; prescriptions and sick notes – red book
- Maintain accurate filing systems and in accordance with filing times
- Receive post and direct as appropriate and arrange collection of post that day
- Ensure that requests for prescriptions are attended to within one working day
- Keep the kitchen area, reception area, and record area clean and tidy; to tidy magazines in the waiting room
- Always ensure confidentiality; do not leave patient details on computer screen or load letters where they can be seen by others. Always follow practice procedures on confidentiality
- Undertake other duties delegated as appropriate

- Ability to cope calmly and efficiently with unexpected difficulties;
- Good speaking voice and smart appearance.

Additional duties

There will be occasions when receptionists will have to cope with awkward situations – often involving anxious patients.

Whatever the situation and however difficult, the receptionist must not show anger to patients but must remain calm, helpful, and pleasant. Apart from an anxious patient, a receptionist will have to deal occasionally with aggressive or angry calls to the practice and visitors with physical difficulties or disabilities.

At all times a receptionist needs to be knowledgeable about the practice services, procedures, and the layout of the premises. This will help her to deal competently and efficiently with patients and other visitors.

Health and safety and security

The practice receptionist will be responsible for looking after visitors to the practice. She should be familiar with safety regulations, the practice health and safety policy, and first aid procedures and also be responsible for recording any accidents occurring in the practice.

Staff in/out book

Many receptionists will be required to provide information about which staff have left the premises and the time they expect to return. This is a very useful record as they will know staff movements. It helps avoid the embarrassing situation of repeatedly having to tell callers they have been unable to contact a particular doctor or member of staff.

8 Staff appraisal and performance review

The use of staff appraisal and performance review is widespread in industry. It has been slower in catching on in general practice. This is possibly because the process is more often associated with larger organisations. In some cases appraisal has been viewed cynically as a formal once-a-year, backward looking review of performance; sometimes associated with salary increases (or even a standstill); sometimes as a ritual ticking off for performance lapses over the previous year. In other cases the process is viewed with extreme reluctance by GPs and practice managers who prefer to treat staff as professional colleagues rather than as subordinates on whom they are entitled to pass judgment.

Practice staff often view appraisal with scepticism and see the process as a rather patronising exercise designed only to humiliate them or punish past omissions or inadequacies in work performance. Yet a properly managed performance appraisal scheme can motivate staff and bring positive benefits to the practice.

Who benefits?

Staff

Appraisal is about effective communication between GPs or practice manager and individual practice staff. It gives the opportunity of planned time to review performance together. The appraisal process can enable staff to:

- Agree on what the job actually consists of
- Have a clear understanding of what is expected of them
- Find out how they are seen to be doing
- Know how they are valued by the practice
- Increase confidence and awareness
- Discuss problems in the job
- Emphasise their own achievements
- Generate their own solutions to problems and accept responsibility for their own development
- Contribute to success – for example, help establish policies, objectives, new services, procedures, etc
- Make the case for regrading, promotion, or salary review
- Discuss training and development needs and agree action
- Agree on a plan for the year ahead.

The practice

Practices that run successful appraisal schemes have found that they have gained:

- Important insights into the work being done
- Greater staff awareness of practice policies and objectives
- Improvements in the planning, control, and monitoring of practice work and activities
- Greater openness in discussions with staff and as a result better employee relations and morale
- More purposeful and regular communications with staff rather than having to rely on a casual chat
- The opportunity to assess training needs
- A better insight into individuals' strengths and weaknesses, their future potential in the job, and any promotional potential
- A more tangible measure of staff performance than relying on judgment about an individual's character
- Staff better able and willing to manage change.

Patients

The services provided to patients will benefit if the practice has well motivated staff whose abilities, talents, and expertise are more effectively harnessed to the practice's aims and objectives. The practice that seeks to identify the strengths and weaknesses of its staff can build on these and is in a better position to analyse problems, to review the quality and range of services, and to develop new thinking and ideas.

Objectives of staff appraisal

Staff appraisals and performance reviews should be a continuous and dynamic cycle. Unlike traditional appraisal systems, which merely look over a 6 to 12 month period, an effective appraisal scheme seeks to:

- Look forward
- Review progress
- Appraise the practice team individually and collectively against a measured standard of performance
- Identify where improvements can be made and where there are obstacles to them
- Train and develop on a continual basis
- Review and reset practice targets.

Making appraisals

Even without having given much thought to formal staff appraisal schemes, many practices will already have been appraising staff. Effectively managed practices will have been continuously – but informally – appraising staff on a day-to-day, or week-to-week basis throughout the year. Developing a formal approach to appraisals requires much care and attention. The skills needed to achieve effective performance appraisal extend beyond somebody having a good system. Knowing how to inform a person about his or her ability (or lack of it) to carry out a particular task is a sensitive exercise, which can either motivate or alienate the employee concerned. The process calls for good communication and interpersonnel skills. The appraiser's attitude will either encourage or discourage an employee's confidence and involvement in the process.

Doing the paperwork

There are many elaborate systems of appraisal available, many of which would be unsuitable for general practice. A practice scheme should not be too elaborate. In designing an appraisal form, provision should be made for:

- Personal details
- Job title
- Job description

- Details of performance against a set of job-related criteria
- A performance rating
- General comments by practice manager or GP
- Comments by the employee
- A plan for development and action.

Job descriptions

What is expected of a person (the tasks and activities to be undertaken) has to be stated. This should be agreed between the parties involved in the appraisal. The practice should have up to date and agreed job descriptions prepared for all staff (see page 4) and this should give a good starting point for the appraisal. The job description can provide a framework against which performance can be monitored and reviewed.

Simpler methods of job appraisal available and which would be suitable in smaller organisations like general practice are the following:

Rating method

This method lists the factors to be assessed, such as quality and output of work, which are then rated on a numerical scale according to level of performance (see box).

The benefit of this kind of system is that it is simple to use and understand. It is, however, highly subjective. (A simple model performance review for a practice receptionist is shown in figure 8.1).

Comparison with objectives

This method allows an employee and practice manager or GP to agree objectives at the beginning of the appraisal period. The

---

Numerical scale showing performance level

1. Outstanding
2. Exceeds requirements of the job
3. Meets the requirements of the job
4. Shows some minor weaknesses
5. Shows some significant weakness
6. Unacceptable

Job Title: Practice receptionist

Appraiser: Practice manager

Note to appraiser Either circle the letter according to the guidance below or by ticking the statement that best describes the apraisee.

Performance guidance that may be used in assessing performance standards:

A = Exceptional. The individual maintains a level of performance well in excess of the requirements of the job.

B = Highly efficient. Good performance that displays an overall level of efficiency that generally meets, and sometimes exceeds, the required standard for the job.

C = Effective. The individual achieves the requirements of the job but sometimes needs guidance to reach this level.

D = Unsatisfactory performance that frequently fails to reach the necessary standard.

E = Poor performance that does not meet the standard expected.

TECHNICAL ABILITIES

Typing	A B C D E
Clerical duties (collating, filing, etc)	A B C D E

Telephone manner (tick as appropriate)
 Always clear and polite _____
 Usually clear and polite _____
 Needs attention _____

Knowledge of software
 Fully comprehensive _____
 Rarely asks for instructions _____
 Sometimes need help _____
 Frequently needs help _____

Personal organisation
 Always well organised _____
 Usually well organised _____
 Sometimes confused _____
 Unmethodical and disordered _____

Tidiness	A B C D E

PERSONAL QUALITIES

Appearance
 Always neat and tidy _____
 Usually neat and tidy _____
 Needs attention _____

Figure 8.1 A simple performance review checklist

Figure 8.1 continued

Punctuality
    Invariably punctual   _____
    Usually on time   _____
    Occasionally late   _____
    Often late   _____

Attitude to work
    Enthusiastic   _____
    Satisfactory   _____
    Lacks effort   _____

Initiative
    Requires very little supervision   _____
    Requires supervision only occasionally   _____
    Sometimes needs to be told what to do   _____
    Frequently needs to be told what to do   _____

Job knowledge
    Fully comprehensive   _____
    Sound knowledge of most aspects of the job   _____
    Sometimes relies on others for information   _____
    Knows only the basic elements   _____
    Unsatisfactory   _____

Speed of work   A   B   C   D   E

Accuracy of work   A   B   C   D   E

Training undertaken or new skills acquired
    Specify details

Disposition
    Copes easily with irate customers
      and stressful situations   _____
    Usually able to cope with
      difficult or stressful situations   _____
    Occasionally becomes irritable   _____
    Liable to fly off the handle   _____

Ability to concentrate   A   B   C   D   E

Reliability (dependability)   A   B   C   D   E

Relationships with superiors and colleagues
    Good   _____
    Satisfactory   _____
    Unsatisfactory (specify on a separate sheet)   _____

Interpersonal communications skills
    Verbal
    Articulate and self-confident   _____
    Generally satisfactory   _____
    Needs attention   _____

Figure 8.1 continued

Written
  Good   _____
  Satisfactory   _____
  Needs attention   _____
Cooperation
  Always works extremely well with other people   _____
  Normally cooperative   _____
  Can sometimes be difficult to work with   _____
  Uncooperative   _____
Further comments
  Specify

subsequent appraisal is based on how far these objectives have been met. This method is more objective than the ratings method because the emphasis is on achievement. It can be more participative because it gives employees the chance to agree their objectives and enables them to carry out a type of self appraisal.

Critical incidents

This method involves a GP or manager reporting and analysing critical incidents that have occurred in the course of an employee's work during the review period. Specific cases of outstandingly good or bad performance are isolated and discussed. Under this method staff may feel that they are continually being spied on as the appraiser is forced to isolate and report significant aspects of the employee's work. This method requires frequent recording and enables an employee's performance to be judged on actual incidents rather than on subjective assessments. The method however can be time-consuming and burdensome.

The free report

This method allows the appraiser to describe an individuals' work performance and behaviour in his or her own words. The appraiser writes what in effect is an essay about the employee, structured in form and length and using criteria selected previously.

Alternatively, an outline structure may be imposed, with

suggested headings for such things as technical competence, communications ability, willingness to cooperate with others, etc, to direct the appraiser's thoughts and comments. The disadvantage of this type of approach is that it requires careful preparation. Busy managers and GPs might leave undone, or treat superficially, this time-consuming activity. The chosen criteria might not be clear or might be inappropriate, which might make comparisons between the performance of one employee and others impossible.

Appraisal interviewing

As with most interviews, successful appraisal interviews should be held in private, in appropriate surroundings, with no interruptions from phones or people, and with sufficient time for a full exploration of the issues raised (see chapter 3). The appraisal interview should cover:

- Detailed reviews of job performance, of specific key objectives aimed for in the review period, of what was achieved, and of how it was achieved
- Identification of any problem areas or "bad news," and discussion of how these can be worked through successfully
- Identification of what the individual can do to improve performance further in difficult job areas
- Identification of what the practice manager or GP can do in terms of training, coaching, counselling, and supporting to enhance future performance
- A review of training progress where appropriate
- Agreement of goals and specific standards to be met in the forthcoming review period
- Discussion of the person's development aspirations and what the practice can contribute to their achievement.

Further reading

Employee Appraisal. Advisory, Conciliatary and Arbitration Service (ACAS) advisory booklet No 11.

9 Drawing up a staff handbook

Clear and well thought out practice policies and procedures are not only important for the efficient running of a practice; they also help improve staff relations and morale by reducing the chance of misunderstandings.

Staff need access to a wealth of practice information about important policies and procedures on such issues as patient confidentiality or handling inquiries from the local newpaper. They also need information about terms and conditions of employment.

But the finest practice policies will have little or no impact unless they are clearly explained to and understood by staff. One of the best ways to achieve this is through a staff handbook.

A handbook will help partners, managers, and staff alike. From time to time aspects of practice policy will be forgotten. What better tool than a handbook to avoid constantly answering the same questions: 'What is the practice policy on accepting a new patient?' or 'What is the current Whitley scale for a receptionist?' Such questions can be covered in a staff handbook.

The actual process of setting out all practice policy in a handbook may well reveal gaping holes in practice procedures or inconsistencies in policy. Compiling a handbook may improve those policies. A staff handbook can also benefit the practice as: (a) a means of meeting legal requirements, and (b) an aid to the practice induction programme for new staff.

Meeting legal requirements

Health and Safety at Work Act, 1974

Employers with five or more employees have a duty to prepare and issue and, as often as is necessary, revise a written statement of their general policy about health and safety at work. The statement should outline the organisation and the arrangements for carrying out the policy, and employers must bring it to the notice of all employees.

Employment Protection (Consolidation) Act, 1978

This provides that certain terms and conditions must be in writing or must refer to a readily accessible document where the terms can be found. Written particulars should include the following:

- Names of the parties
- Date of commencement of employment and any continuous employment that counts
- Job title or brief description of job
- Salary and payment intervals and how salary is calculated
- Place of work (including any branch surgery)
- Hours of work
- Any sickness benefit
- Any holiday entitlement
- Notice terms
- Any pension scheme and whether or not a contracted out certificate is in force
- Any disciplinary rules
- A person to whom employees may appeal if they are dissatisfied with any disciplinary decision and to whom they may take a grievance.

Remember that unwritten policies and procedures (often interpreted as custom and practice) could be used in legal proceedings. It is therefore a good idea to have them documented in a way that the practice wants them interpreted, not in the way an industrial tribunal might interpret them.

An aid to induction

The early induction of new staff into the practice is the final part of a successful recruitment process and the first part of a successful retention programme. Any induction programme should help a new member of staff adapt to the requirements of the job and the practice's working arrangements.

A staff handbook can aid the successful induction of staff by providing them with a useful checklist of practice issues, detailing such matters as the work of the practice, conditions of service, rules and standards, patient services, and staff benefits.

Contents of a handbook

A staff handbook should begin with a brief 'welcome to the practice' letter (fig 9.1). This can serve several purposes, including greeting new employees as they begin their first day at work and establishing the practice philosophy ("our practice is

---

Dear Mrs Smith

We would like to welcome you on to the staff of the Glendale Health Centre.

As a practice we strive to provide the highest quality service to all our patients. We hope that, as a member of staff, you will be able to contribute to the achievement of this aim.

We encourage all staff to play a full and active part in practice activities and to attend our regular practice meetings on Friday mornings. Also, we encourage staff to take part in appropriate training courses and events. Mrs Bloggs, practice manager, will be only too happy to discuss with you our staff training policy.

We hope that the accompanying handbook will answer any questions you may have about practice policies and procedures. Most issues will also be covered during the course of your induction programme. Nevertheless, should you wish to discuss any aspect of either practice policy or your employment, do not hesitate to contact one of us.

We look forward to a long and fruitful association and hope you will enjoy working with us.

Yours sincerely

Drs Jones, Williams, and Gardner

Figure 9.1 Specimen "welcome from the partners" letter

forward looking and aims to achieve the highest level of patient satisfaction").

Background details, such as practice activities, number of doctors, staff details and arrangements with the FHSA, may follow the introductory letter, but the bulk of the handbook will be a brief description or explanation of practice policies and procedures. Before beginning the task of writing a handbook, consult the partners and other staff to pick up ideas and additional items which might otherwise be overlooked. A checklist of things to include could cover:

- Employment matters: employment status (full time, part time, or job share); salary policy (method, interval, and deductions); hours of work (including lunch breaks); flexibility arrangements; notice periods; holidays (how they are calculated, and restrictions); overtime working; performance or profit related supplements; pensions; sickness absence (reporting requirements, statutory sickness pay); special leave; maternity or paternity leave; lateness reporting; change of personal circumstances; employee benefits (Christmas bonuses and leave); termination of employment; and discipline and grievance handling.
- Practice policies: induction of new staff; health and safety; fire routines and first aid; conduct and appearance; patient confidentiality; security; staff training; patient complaints; retirement; equal opportunities; trade union membership; staff appraisal; and smoking.
- Others: identification (name tags); cash handling procedures; contact with press; staff suggestions; practice leaflets and information; noticeboards; parking arrangements; layout of practice premises; and facilities for patients (disabled, etc).

Depending on the size of the handbook, it may be helpful to include an index page for ease of reference. After choosing the topics to include and drafting the text, it is a good idea to test it out for user friendliness on a member of staff, one of the partners, or a friend.

The final product

A handbook will not be much use to the practice if staff do not read it or if, having read it, they do not understand it. So you have to make it attractive enough for staff to want to read it, and it must be written to be understood. Do not sound pompous and avoid legal or technical jargon.

How attractive you make it depends on your budget. Usually, producing a handbook will involve using a word processor, a photocopier, and a stapler. Even on a very small budget the presentation could be enhanced with illustrations, diagrams, or even cartoons (many computer software packages have a facility for these).

Practice policies, procedures, and the law are always changing, so a handbook must be kept up to date. Larger practices might consider a loose-leaf handbook.

Providing practice information in a single document should make a positive contribution to the overall running and image of the practice, at the same time helping staff to understand the running of the practice and identify with its aims and objectives.

Further reading

The Company Handbook. Advisory, Conciliatory and Arbitration Service (ACAS) advisory booklet No. 9.
Handbook for General Practice Staff. Available free to members from BMA regional offices.

10 Organising staff training

Staff training should be a top priority for GPs. General practice has undergone major changes in recent years. Changes like fundholding and the NHS market inevitably affect the way work is done in general practice and may mean that some if not all staff must acquire new knowledge and skills. Responsibility for meeting operational changes in the practice is a major part of every manager's duty; retraining is vital to achieve this. Training not only benefits the practice but also is a means of improving and developing the knowledge, skills, and attitudes of individual staff (see box overleaf).

Who needs training?

New staff should always be offered induction training in order to familiarise them with practice procedures and policies. The importance of induction training cannot be overemphasised, especially where young employees are concerned. New staff rarely bring to the job the full range of knowledge and skills required, and they will usually require training in the skills and knowledge needed to do the new job.

The practice selection procedure should identify the gaps where new staff will require training. As far as existing staff are concerned, any training needs will have been identified through the practice appraisal system. A good job appraisal scheme will identify any weaknesses in work performance, whether owing to deficiencies in the employees themselves or to changes in the job.

Benefits of training

For the practice

- Reduction of learning time and costs
- Improvement in job performance – for example, in terms of quality of work and work done on time
- Less supervision
- Increased patient satisfaction
- Reduced staff turnover by increased job satisfaction
- Better recruitment and selection; training opportunities help to attract the right type of employees

For the employee

- Improves job security
- Improves promotion prospects
- Greater job satisfaction
- Greater skill transferability

What training is to be done?

To train staff effectively it is first necessary to decide in detail what specific knowledge and skills the job requires, what skills and knowledge individuals already possess, and what gaps in knowledge and skills training can fill. The systematic approach to the identification of training needs means looking at existing and up to date job descriptions and asking the job holder about the nature of the work. A practice manager will have an appreciation of all jobs, but it is worth checking the job holders' perceptions of their tasks. The next step entails identifying the skills and knowledge already possessed by the job holder. This may be obvious with new staff with whom knowledge and skills will have been discussed at interview. With existing staff the job appraisal scheme is the best way of establishing the range and knowledge of skills held by an individual. Without a formal appraisal you will need to establish an individual's training requirements in a one to one interview and try to identify their strengths and weaknesses. Meeting training needs is all about bridging the gap between these two stages.

How to train

Not only are managers responsible for training staff but in many respects they are the best people to do the training. They know the job, know their staff, and have a direct interest in their successful performance. The method adopted will depend on the numbers to be trained, the complexity of the work to be done, the difficulties of the training process, and the resources available to the manager. Training can be arranged in a number of ways:

- On the job (on site, desk training) – assignments or projects, coaching, job instruction, job rotation
- Off the job, in house – internal courses, programmed instruction, package programmes
- Off the job, external – outside courses, correspondence courses, guided reading, television and radio programmes.

Common methods of training

- *Coaching* – involves managers giving staff carefully planned tasks and continuous appraisal and counselling.
- *Job rotation* – involves planned experience programmes whereby staff regularly change their jobs, enabling them to acquire an overall understanding of the practice.
- *External courses* – these can provide opportunities to acquire technical and professional qualifications and training in subjects of which there is no knowledge or experience within the practice. They are useful for meeting specific needs when numbers are too small for an internal course. Such courses provide an ideal opportunity for trainees to compare notes and, hopefully to pick up tips on "best practice."
- *Internal courses* – can be organised within the practice or can involve participants from a neighbouring practice. In some cases it may be appropriate to invite external speakers or trainees. The advantage of internal courses is that they can be tailored to meet specific needs, are relatively inexpensive, and can take place at a time convenient to the practice. An induction programme is essential in any practice and can take place on this basis.
- *Packaged training programmes* – usually consist of a training manual, exercises, and audiovisual aids and therefore require access to equipment such as a tape recorder or overhead projector. They are available on many subjects, including

employment law, staff appraisal, customer service, staff selection, and problem solving techniques. These programmes can be very useful to managers because all the hard work (such as collecting the material, designing the programme, and producing an instructional manual) has already been done. They are usually expensive but can be shared with other practices and they are suitable for group training sessions.

- *Role playing* – is a form of learning by doing. It allows trainees to see issues from other perspectives and point of view, albeit in artificial circumstances. This method of training is a good way of helping trainees to recognise their own strengths and weaknesses by allowing them to make mistakes and then correct them without incurring serious "real life" consequences. The main disadvantage is that role playing can expose sensitive trainees to destructive criticism and make them "turn off". Nevertheless, it is a good way of training staff in such matters as patient relations, telephone techniques, communication skills, and chairmanship.

Planning a training programme

Whichever method of training is chosen, the aim should always be to inspire action rather than bombard the trainee with knowledge and facts. In planning a programme of training it is helpful to ask, and answer, the following questions:

- Who is to be trained – number and type of employee?
- Why are they to be trained – what are the training objectives? What should be taught?
- How should training be done – what methods should be used?
- Who should do the training?
- When can it be done – length and frequency?
- Where will it be done – location?
- How will it be assessed?

In designing any training programme, consideration should be given to the following points:

- *Sequence* – A training programme should follow a chronological sequence and identify the order of priorities. It is often helpful to identify common or related items in the sequence.

- *Load and pace* – How much training trainees can absorb, and how quickly they can learn, should be considered.
- *Variety* – Variety is essential in successful training programmes, not only in the subject matter but also in the methods of delivering the programme.
- *Feedback* – With feedback the trainee finds out whether the course has been satisfactory or not. Sometimes this will be obvious because of the quality of the performance, particularly with physical skill learning. Some feedback from the coach or trainer can help to distinguish levels of satisfaction and analyse what went wrong, how it could be avoided, what needs more practice, what to do next, and so on.

Evaluating the training programme

The final part of planning any training programme for staff is to assess whether the time and money invested has been worth it. An effective evaluation of the programme is important to ensure that the standard of training is satisfactory and to help to assess the future training needs of practice staff. As a practice manager you should ask the following questions:

- Did the results meet the training objectives – that is, did performance improve?
- What benefits accrued to the practice?
- Were there any spinoffs over and above the objectives set?
- How much did it cost?
- What revision needs to be made to the training programme in the future?

Your starting point in evaluating the training should be feedback from participants, such as a questionnaire. In many cases evaluation will be fairly straightforward. The value of a word processing course, for example, should be easily demonstratable. The job of evaluating the training effect becomes more difficult with more complex jobs.

Training or development

A distinction needs to be drawn between training and development. Training usually refers to specific activities geared to improving the skills and knowledge needed to do a particular job. An example is training to use the new practice desk top computer system. Development, on the other hand, usually refers to less distinct objectives related to longer term, less easily definable aims that are associated with personal improvement. An example would be a development programme for leadership. The emphasis in this chapter has been on planning training programmes, but GPs and practice managers should also take into account the development needs of their staff. Success in general practice depends on the quality of the people working in it. Training and development of staff has a vital role.

11 Designing a staff salary structure

Many practices are having to give serious thought to devising their own staff salary structures. The practice staff scheme introduced in 1990, which replaced the ancillary staff scheme, significantly changed how practices receive reimbursement for the cost of employing practice staff. With greater family health services authority discretion over the range and number of staff attracting reimbursement, practices must adopt a more flexible and innovative approach to staff salaries. Whitley Council staff rates, which have traditionally been used as a yardstick for pay scales in general practice, may have a limited shelf life. The government makes no secret of its wish to see national pay bargaining replaced with local pay determination.

Another factor that puts staff pay policy at the top of the agenda is the changing labour force. In 1982–3 just over 900 000 young people left school to start work; by 1992–3 this total had declined to around 630 000. Overall, by the year 2000 employers will have one million fewer young people available for recruitment than there were in 1990. The problem facing all employers will be exacerbated by the fact that more than half of those leaving school in the mid-1990s will have no proper qualifications when they leave. All these factors mean that practices will increasingly be required to devise their own pay policies to attract the right staff, instead of relying on centrally prescribed pay scales and grades.

A practice's ability to recruit and retain the right people will be largely determined by salary considerations. When devising a structured policy on pay, GPs must take account of many factors that influence pay – the nature of the job, market values, performance, and motivating factors. Before delving into the area of salary policies, however, a cautionary word is advisable. Pay is probably the most important part of any employment relationship. It is also (a) a major element of a GP's expenses in the day to day running of the practice, (b) one of the most important factors in attracting and retaining practice staff of the highest calibre, (c) an influence on how staff will work and on their levels of motivation, and (d) a potential source of conflict between employer and employee. With these things in mind it is always advisable to seek specialist advice and guidance on matters relating to salary issues.

Types of salary structure

Before embarking on either devising a salary structure or revising an existing one, GPs should ask several basic questions:

What can the practice afford? This will be determined largely by the practice income and the level of reimbursement from the family health services authority.

What level of pay will attract suitable candidates? Information on current rates of pay obtainable from local newspapers as well as from the specialist medical press. Local colleges are also useful sources of information about local rates.

What level of pay will ensure that staff stay with the practice? Pay is not the only motivating force for people at work. Other factors are important, including the nature of the work, other terms and conditions of employment, working relationships, and environment. Nevertheless pay is crucially important.

What differentials will exist? You need to be able to justify the fairness of differentials between different grades of staff.

What does the law require? You must ensure that you pay equal rates and provide the same conditions to men and women who are doing the same work.

The best type of salary system is one that has been carefully selected to take account of the needs of the practice and those of its employees. It is important that a system has the commitment of staff and, when possible, is developed and maintained in consultation with them. Many forms of salary systems exist, but they can usually be classified as time related or performance based.

Time related staff salaries

Paying the rate for the job is the simplest and most common system. Time related salary structures provide either (a) a single rate for the job or (b) a defined range within which indiviudal rates may vary, according to age or length of service.

Time rates provide employees with a set rate per hour, week, or month. The rate need not be the same for all working hours. Premium rates may be paid for overtime. Pay is usually related to the length of time worked and assumes a basic level of performance. Systems based on time rates are usually cheaper to operate. They are easily understood and are less prone to dispute than performance or incentive schemes. The problem is that there is no direct link between pay and performance, so staff need close supervision to maintain acceptable performance to the levels and standards you require.

Whatever staff pay system you decide on as being most suitable for your practice, it is essential to ensure that employees are involved in the process. Sounding out their views and opinions will help you to arrive at the right system and will save time, trouble, and expense.

Incremental salary scales

Incremental salary scales are common in the public sector. With this pay system, a minimum salary is usually linked to qualifying criteria – which may include a staff member's age, qualifications, and experience – for entry to a specific grade. Progress within the grade is then by annual increments of defined amounts and is thus largely independent of any given performance criteria. Under this arrangement the only way in which outstanding performance can be rewarded is by offering double increments or promotion. In the NHS, efforts have been made to move away from the rigidity of incremental salary scales by adding performance related supplements. Incremental scales are rarely used in business and industry as they are seen as being too rigid.

Performance related salary scales

Most private sector organisations use some form of performance or incentive based scheme. Like all systems, performance related pay is inextricably linked to employee relations and can have a considerable effect on efficiency. There is no hard evidence that performance related pay improves individual or business

73

performance, but it can help to emphasise the importance of effective job performance as well as to motivate employees. In general practice it can be more complicated to administer and probably more expensive to operate. Most systems rely on regular, systematic staff appraisal – a good way to manage staff if carried out sensibly, but not universally used in general practice. Appraisals can motivate staff and help improve performance by identifying strengths and weaknesses, high-lighting training needs, and assessing promotion potential. An existing staff appraisal scheme could form the basis of a performance related pay structure. Advocates of the system point to certain advantages, but the practice should also be aware that there are disadvantages (see box).

Performance related pay systems take many forms and include:

Performance related pay

The pros

- It encourages and supports a culture of high performance
- Resources can be better directed to recognising effort and achievement and to rewarding and retaining valued staff
- It can promote employee involvement and commitment
- Spinoffs include improvements in quality of services provided
- It motivates all staff

The cons

- If staff and management relationships are characterised by lack of trust, or staff are not ready or willing to embrace change, performance related pay could adversely affect employee relations
- It can demotivate staff and lead to distrust. Any credible scheme must be seen as fair and objective; targets must be specific and achievable
- Some experts argue that individual performance related schemes hinder teamwork and cooperation
- It may not greatly affect work performance. Critics say that pay is not the only motivating force at work. Challenge, working environment, and job security are often shown to be more important to staff

---

- *Linking increases, within the normal pay scales, to performance* This is the most common system; progression depends on achieving satisfactory performance
- *Performance pay increases above the maximum scale point* This scheme retains an incremental scale but adds a performance supplement
- *Increases to single point salary* Used where there is no incremental pay scale and no automatic annual salary increase. Salary is subject to annual review and is usually determined by individual or group performance in the past year
- *Lump sum performance payments* Different levels of performance generate varying bonuses. These can be added to most existing salary systems
- *Group based schemes* Performance pay can be applied to groups and the supplements divided among all staff, equally or in an agreed ratio. Group schemes are used where it isn't possible to attribute individual performance.

Profit related pay structures

As with performance based schemes, profit related pay is intended to link the practice's performance with staff pay. In an effort to promote profit related schemes, the government introduced tax relief for profit related pay in 1987. GPs are currently barred from offering their employees tax free profit

---

Steps to follow in devising or revising pay systems

1 Involve all employees. Sounding out staff opinion will help you design the right pay system and will save you time, trouble, and expense
2 Identify weaknesses in the existing system and eradicate faults
3 If possible, revise or strengthen the existing salary system
4 Consider what factors you need to build into the system. Is a higher priority to be given to quality or output? Do staff want an incentive element? How will performance be assessed and standards set?
5 Pave the way by briefing staff
6 Maintain and review the system
7 Seek expert advice and guidance before embarking on the exercise

---

related pay, which involves setting up a special inland revenue registered scheme, because general practice is supported by public funds. One consolation is, some say, that pay is not the only motivating force at work. Challenge, working environment, and job security are often shown to be more important to staff.

12 Absent friends – managing sickness absence

In 1993 employers lost an average of eight working days in sick leave for every member of the UK workforce. According to recent figures on sickness absence levels published by the CBI (Confederation of British Industry), this represents 3·5% of working time. Sick leave is estimated to cost British industry £11m a year. Public sector employees took more time off sick in 1993 than private sector workers, averaging 10 days compared with $7\frac{1}{2}$ days. According to the CBI and other surveys, organisations that operate absence management policies report significantly fewer days lost than organisations without a policy.

Staff absenteeism poses practical problems for the running of any general practice. It is costly in terms of providing temporary cover, administering any practice sick pay scheme, and increased overtime costs. It increases pressure on other staff and on administration time because of rota arrangements having to be changed. It also disrupts the flow of work. High absentee rates can affect staff morale and motivation as well as job satisfaction generally.

Yet most practices do not have an effective policy to combat absenteesim, many GPs are too embarrassed to address the issue. Because absenteesim is often a visible sign of employees "voting with their feet", admitting to high levels of absenteeism may be seen as tantamount to being perceived as a bad employer. Others treat absenteeism – like the weather – as an act of God that has to be endured, rather than an organisational problem capable of being solved. Dealing effectively with absence requires continuous and coordinated efforts between GPs and practice managers.

Measuring sickness absence

You cannot manage a problem until you can measure it. Accurate recording and monitoring of information is the foundation of an effective absence policy. Measuring levels and frequency of absence should not be a problem for most practices: several techniques that are commonly used in business are available and can help.

The standard formula used for calculating absence rates is:

No of days lost ÷ Total no of working days × 100

This is called the "lost time rate" and measures the severity of the problem – for example, if an employee has been "off sick" for 25 working days (out of a total of 230) the lost time rate is: $25 \div 230 \times 100 = 10.8\%$.

The total time lost may be caused by one or two employees having been away for long periods, or several for short spells. The "frequency rate" shows how widespread the problem is by highlighting the average number of spells of absence per employee, irrespective of the length of each spell, as follows:

No of spells of absence ÷ no of employees × 100

Individual frequency rates can be calculated to monitor the number of employees absent at all during the period:

No of employees absent once or more ÷ No of employees × 100

For example, in a practice that employs 15 staff, during a 12 month period four employees were off sick: one was off twice, two were away three times, and one was away once, which gives a total of six spells of absence. The frequency rate was $6 \div 15 \times 100 = 40\%$; and the individual frequency rate was $4 \div 15 \times 100 = 27\%$.

Using these measures will help identify the scale of the problem and identify specific topics needing attention.

Causes of absenteeism

Popular reasons for missing work include domestic problems, a death in the family, doctors' or dentists' appointments, or fear of catching something from an already infectious colleague. Quite often the reasons for absenteeism may be related to work itself or to the practice (see box opposite).

Reasons for absenteeism

Related to the job

- An employee finding the job boring or repetitious
- Poor organisation and inefficient systems of work
- Lack of equipment

Related to management

- Being perceived as unfair
- Being too autocratic
- Being perceived as incompetent
- Not treating employees as individuals
- Being unable to make decisions
- Being too aggressive
- Being afraid of confrontation

Related to the individual

- Personality clashes with the manager, partners, or colleagues
- Inability to do the job
- Being overqualified for the job and therefore finding it boring or frustrating
- Being unable to cope with the pressure
- Being lazy or workshy

Controlling absenteeism

Simply by identifying the problem means you are some way towards solving it. One of the factors that influence individuals' decisions to stay away from work is often whether or not their absence will be questioned or even noticed. Keeping records, and monitoring patterns, of absence (for example, identifying trends, such as whether absence rates are higher for an individual on a Monday morning) is therefore important.

You need to distinguish between long term absence through ill health and persistent or intermittent short term absences.

Dealing with long term sickness

Dealing with long term sickness in any small organisation or business is difficult and traumatic. There is usually a conflict between dealing sensitively and compassionately with a possibly long serving member of staff who is seriously ill and the need to ensure the continuing and effective operation of the practice. The issues to consider in dealing with long term sickness are as follows:

- Can the practice afford to carry on without a replacement or reorganisation of the practice?
- Is a return to work likely?
- Will there be a full recovery?
- Could the practice reorganise or redesign the job?
- Is there an alternative job available (with retraining if necessary)?
- How old is the employee, and how long has he or she been with the practice?
- What costs are being incurred by the absence?
- Is early retirement feasible or acceptable?
- Have all the possibilities been discussed with the employee concerned?

Legally, a dismissal on the grounds of long term sickness can be fair provided that a proper procedure has been followed. Disciplinary warnings here are not appropriate. If the time comes when employment can no longer be guaranteed then the employee must be told. The position of the practice should be explained. Only after full consideration has been given to the issues above should dismissal be contemplated. Remember you may have to satisfy an industrial tribunal that you acted fairly and reasonably.

Persistent short term absences

Short term absences are usually as disruptive as they are unpredictable. A certain amount of short term sickness is to be expected, but frequent absence may indicate general ill health requiring medical investigation. This needs to be distinguished from cases where an employee is "swinging the lead" (that is, taking frequent odd days off and giving illness as the excuse). Tribunals take a different view of this type of absence and tend to consider it as a question of an employee's conduct (for example, is it an abuse of a generous sick pay arrangement?). Nevertheless, the same rules of fairness and reasonableness apply as in any other dismissal case. In absenteeism cases where there is doubt about someone's medical condition, you should get the employee's permission to obtain an independent medical report. This should then be discussed with the employee. Remember that medical certificates by themselves may not present a total picture, neither do they provide a prognosis. What is needed is a fair review of the attendance record and the reasons for it, appropriate warnings to the employee of the likely consequences if there is no improvement; and giving the employee the opportunity to explain his or her record. The practice should adopt a clear policy on absence reporting procedures and how to deal with persistent absentees. A suggested policy is set out in the box.

Model absence management policy

Recording procedures

First day of absence

- Employee must notify practice manager/GP direct, before 10am, of absence.
- Give reasons for absence and likely duration.

Absence 4-7 days

- A self certification form, marked "confidential", should be submitted in accordance with established procedure on the first day back at work. It should be noted that "sick" or "unwell" is insufficient information.

Absence 7 days or more

- Employee must submit a medical certificate from GP.

When absenteeism becomes a problem

Stage one – trigger points

- Employee has been absent on four or more other separate occasions in a rolling 12-month period, or
- Employee has been absent four consecutive weeks, or
- Employee has had 14 days' absence from the practice in a rolling 12-month period.

(whichever occurs first, go to stage two.)

Stage two – counselling

- Discuss attendance record with employee.
- Give employee a copy of record. Agree accuracy.
- Identify number of days absent, spells of absence, and reasons for absence from work.

- Explain effect of absence on practice and other staff.

- Identify possible reasons for absence: job related, management or practice related, personal, or underlying and undiagnosed medical problem.

- Discuss methods of improving absence record.

- Agree a date for reviewing the situation.

Stage three – no improvement

- Interview employee

- Employee is allowed to be accompanied by a friend or colleague if this is requested.

- Point out that absence record is unacceptable.

- Is an independent medical report required?

- Explain that if there is no improvement this may lead to disciplinary measures.

- Keep a report of the meeting.

Stage four – warning
    If a warning letter is necessary, this should be given to the employee after a formal interview (with a friend or colleague present if requested).

Stage five – disciplinary proceedings
    If absences continue, further warning may be necessary in line with the practice disciplinary procedures (first and final written warnings, etc, see chapter 14)

Stage six – dismissal considered
    As for practice disciplinary procedures.

This policy covers: unauthorised absence, uncertified sickness, an unacceptable level of certified sickness, unacceptably frequent certified sickness, and unacceptably frequent lateness.

Further reading

Absence. Advisory, Conciliatory and Arbitration Service (ACAS) advisory booklet No 5.

13 Dealing with poor performance

Performance management is an integral part of a practice manager's role. A practice's income is now directly associated with the performance of all practice staff. Practices are being forced to deal with poor performers, and dismissals associated with poor performance are being decided increasingly before industrial tribunals. There is a sliding scale of poor or unacceptable performance ranging from non-cooperation to a total lack of ability to do a job. Often a manager's expectations of an employee's potential are not fulfilled, or long-serving employees are no longer able to fulfil the more demanding tasks expected of them.

The starting point in all cases of poor performance is to identify the problem. Although in most cases it is obvious, it is important that you actually point to something as a guide to required performance. Sources of information about expected standards of work performance would include contracts of employment, job descriptions, and practice standards and procedures. Often expectations of performance are communicated to staff informally through practice meetings and training sessions. Collecting accurate information about the actual performance of staff is important. Sources of information here would include personnel files and records, time sheets, sickness and absence records, complaints from patients, etc. Comparisons between staff might also give an indication of actual performance (for example, the amount of unfinished work, wastage, and number of complaints).

Role of staff appraisal

According to most personnel specialists, the appraisal interview is one of the most effective mechanisms by which an organisation can keep its staff interested, motivated, and committed, as well as providing a regular assessment of an employee's performance, potential, and development needs (see box). This appraisal is an opportunity to take an overall view of work content, loads, and volume, to look back on what has been achieved during the previous period and agree objectives for the next.

How to conduct an appraisal interview

- Create a relaxed, informal atmosphere
- State objectives of the exercise
- Explain the procedures involved – that is, forms, etc
- Explain how you wish to conduct the interview
- Get the employee to assess his performance first
- Use open-ended questions to get a discussion going
- Probe if details are missed or employee speaks in generalities
- Ensure that your review covers all the key areas of the job, the standards, and any short term priority tasks
- Make your assessment known to the person
- Discuss any points arising from your assessment
- Praise for work well done
- Point out areas for improvement and the reasons for them
- Say how you think these areas can be improved
- Encourage
- Summarise from time to time
- Get employee to give views on his or her future development
- Discuss future training needs and development
- Finalise the discussion by a quick overall review of the interview
- State what will happen to any action plans such as attendance on a course
- Show what will happen to the notes taken
- End the interview on a positive note

Reasons for poor performance

Using an appraisal system will help identify the gap between the required standard of work performance and the actual work performance of an individual. If such a gap is apparent then the next stage is to establish the reasons behind the poor performance. The three most common reasons for poor performance are:

(1) Personal reasons such as insufficient intellectual ability, emotional stability, health, or domestic or family circumstances
(2) Organisational reasons such as poor management organisation, lack of training opportunities, unclear instructions, poor job design, poor pay, lack of planning, or poor discipline at work
(3) Individual characteristics such as personality clashes at work, lack of motivation, poor understanding of the job, lack of confidence, or poor integration with the practice team.

In many cases a problem can be traced to poor or badly thought out recruitment procedures. Careful recruitment, selection, and training are essential if the risk of poor performance is to be minimised. When new staff start work the following principles should be observed:

• The standard of work required should be explained, and staff should be left in no doubt about what is expected of them. Clearly work standards must be realistic and measurable
• Where job descriptions are prepared they should convey accurately the main purpose and scope of each job and the tasks involved
• New staff should be made aware of the conditions that are attached to any probation period
• The consequences of any failure to meet the required standards should be explained
• When an employee is promoted, the consequences of failing to "make the grade" in the new job should be explained.

Dealing with poor performance

The most powerful reinforcer of unacceptable performance is to do nothing. A problem should be tackled with a view to

Points to consider

- Setting joint goals – Jointly agree specific goals together with a date to review performance

- Give additional training – Establish a reasonable programme of on-the-job training to help bridge the performance gap

- Deal with any source of dissatisfaction – If possible, remedy any source of dissatisfaction with conditions at work or pay, or at least explain why it is not possible to address the specific problems

- Reorganise or redesign the job – If the problem is associated with the nature of the job to be done try to reorganise the work to redesign its content

- Improve communication – If the message isn't getting through try to improve the clarity of the communication. Look at your management systems

- Use peer group pressure – Would pressure from colleagues be a more effective way to get a person to change or improve performance?

improving performance; punitive measures such as disciplinary procedures should be used only as a last resort and only when other measures will not work. Poor performance must be tackled at an early stage. A practice should not tolerate poor performance because it is too much trouble to deal with or in the hope that it might get better by itself. Usually it will not, and it should be remembered that the long term poor performer is often the most difficult person to deal with.

Once the reason, or reasons, for the poor performance have been established, ways of dealing with it will suggest themselves. This is best done by setting realistic goals for improvement, dicussing what additional resources will be provided in the way of clear instructions and training, and arranging a date for reviewing the performance (see box).

Disciplinary procedures and poor performance

According to a recent survey, poor standards and poor performance are the second most common cause of disciplinary action at work. In law, a lack of ability to do a job is a potentially fair reason for dismissal. In every case, however, it is essential that the causes of poor performance are fully investigated. In the event of industrial tribunal procedures, a practice would be expected to produce some evidence of poor performance. The following guidelines will help identify the cause of poor performance and how to ensure that appropriate action is taken:

- The employee should be asked for an explanation for the poor performance and the explanation checked (for example, pressure of work, domestic problems, etc)
- If the problem is lack of required skills the employee should, wherever practicable, be helped through training and be given reasonable time to reach the required standard of performance
- Factors that should be considered in determining the period allowed for improvement should include the person's length of service, their previous performance, and the extent to which he or she is functioning below standard
- If, despite encouragement and assistance, the employee is unable to reach the required standard of performance, consideration should be given to finding suitable alternative work
- When alternative work is not available the position should be fully explained before any disciplinary action or dismissal is contemplated
- An employee should not normally be dismissed because of poor performance unless warnings and a chance to improve have been given
- If the main reason for the poor performance is the changing nature of the job, the practice might consider whether the situation could possibly be treated as a redundancy matter rather than an ability or conduct issue.

14 Handling disciplinary issues

The thought of carrying out disciplinary action against a member of staff stikes fear and apprehension into most GPs. Flawed or inappropriate disciplinary procedures increasingly form the basis of industrial tribunal proceedings involving practice staff (see box 1).

Box 1 – Disciplinary action and constructive dismissal

Case history
    A nurse employed for five years by a practice was subject to disciplinary proceedings. Her behaviour over the previous two years had been disruptive and had undermined the practice manager's role. The doctors held a disciplinary meeting which resulted in a written warning. The nurse subsequently resigned and claimed constructive dismissal. An industrial tribunal decided that the disciplinary proceedings were flawed. Even though no formal right of appeal had been given, the tribunal felt that this would have been impossible as all the partners had signed the warning letter, thereby denying the nurse any effective right of appeal. Furthermore, the practice manager had been involved in all stages of the proceedings, which meant, in the tribunal's view she had acted as "judge, jury, and prosecutor." Moreover, the practice had not conducted a fair and reasonable hearing in accordance with natural justice or the practice's disciplinary procedure. The tribunal found that the nurse had been unfairly dismissed and awarded compensation against the practice.

Close working relationships with staff often make it difficult for GPs to adopt the more detached and formal approach that is required when a disciplinary matter has to be tackled. Recent tribunal cases show the need for GPs to handle disciplinary matters with irreproachable care and fairness and in accordance with established good practice.

Taking disciplinary action

There are four basic principles involved.

- *Acting promptly* – Many employment problems can be solved if they are dealt with at an early stage. Talking about a problem as soon as it arises is essential, as is the need to gather the facts of the incident or problem, together with any supporting evidence. Notes should always be taken of matters that may result in any kind of disciplinary action.
- *Consistency* – This is fundamental; inconsistent treatment or behaviour can undermine a GP's or practice manager's authority, as well as cause resentment and a sense of being singled out.
- *Predictability* – Practice staff should know what the rules are (these should be spelt out in the staff handbook) and the consequences of not following them. People are more likely to follow the rules when they are familiar and understood and when the consequences of not doing so are known.
- *Tackling the problem and not the person* – The focus of any disciplinary action should be on the problem (for example, breach or practice rules) rather than the person (that is, it should be an issue of specific behaviour or action rather than a character or personality defect on the part of the employee). When the rules are known and understood the employee will be more likely to accept the consequences of a breach of rules.

Establishing and following good practice

In no other area of practice management is it as necessary to go by the book. However well justified taking disciplinary action is, failure to follow proper procedures could land the practice in front of an industrial tribunal. Good practice in disciplinary matters is based on the ACAS code of practice. Although this is not a legally binding document, failure to follow what is regarded as good practice is likely to result in the loss of any case before an industrial tribunal. A practice disciplinary policy should cover (a) disciplinary rules (clearly not every potential matter can be covered but it is important for employees to know which acts and omissions could result in disciplinary action) and (b) procedures, which describe the process by which disciplinary matters will be dealt with. Features of a fair disciplinary procedure have been recommended by ACAS (see box 2).

In every case GPs should ensure that their procedures and

Box 2 – Disciplinary procedure recommended by ACAS

(1) Purpose and scope
The company's aim is to encourage improvement in individual conduct. This procedure sets out the action which will be taken when disciplinary rules are breached.

(2) Principles
(a) The procedure is designed to establish the facts quickly and to deal consistently with disciplinary issues. No disciplinary action will be taken until the matter has been fully investigated.
(b) At every stage employees will have the opportunity to state their case and be represented, if they wish, at the hearings by a shop steward if appropriate, or by a fellow employee.
(c) Employees have the right to appeal against any disciplinary penalty.

(3) Procedure
Stage 1 - oral warning
If conduct or performance is unsatisfactory, the employee will be given a formal ORAL WARNING, which will be recorded. The warning will be disregarded after . . . months' satisfactory service.

Stage 2 - written warning
If the offence is serious, if there is no improvement in standards, or if a further offence occurs, a WRITTEN WARNING will be given which will include the reason for the warning and a note that, if there is no improvement after . . . months, a FINAL WRITTEN WARNING will be given.

Stage 3 - final written warning
If conduct or performance is still unsatisfactory, A FINAL WRITTEN WARNING will be given making it clear that any recurrence of the offence or other serious misconduct within a period of . . . months will result in dismissal.

Box 2 continued

Stage 4 - dismissal
If there is no satisfactory improvement or if further serious misconduct occurs, the employee will be DISMISSED.

(4) Gross misconduct
If, after investigation, it is confirmed that an employee has committed an offence of the following nature (the list is not exhaustive), the normal consequence will be dismissal:

theft, damage to company property, fraud, incapacity for work due to being under the influence of alcohol or illegal drugs, physical assualt, or gross insubordination.

While the alleged gross misconduct is being investigated the employee may be suspended, during which time he or she will be paid the normal hourly rate. Any decision to dismiss will be taken by the employer only.

(5) Appeals
An employee who wishes to appeal against any disciplinary decision must do so to the employer within two working days. The employer will hear the appeal and decide the case as impartially as possible.

---

policies comply with ACAS guidance. This means: (a) setting out the rules in writing and making sure that all staff receive a copy (these could be incorporated into the practice staff handbook); (b) making sure that the rules, as well as the consequences of disregarding them, are clear and unambiguous; (c) applying the rules fairly and consistently; (d) ensuring that all the circumstances (for example, any mitigating or extenuating factors) have been properly taken into account; (e) not allowing a dismissal to occur without the sanction of other partners (or in accordance with the provisions of the partnership agreement); (f) keeping records of all oral and written warnings (these will be vital if tribunal proceedings follow any dismissal); (g) acting reasonably and not applying rules too rigidly (for example, not enforcing rules suddenly when there has been a degree of laxity in the past); (h) being specific; ensuring that warnings are not ambiguous or left open to misinterpretation (for example, "We expect you to turn up for work at 9.00 am" rather than "We want an improvement in your timekeeping"); (i) making clear what action the employee is expected to take and what help the

91

Box 3 – Stages in a disciplinary interview

(1) Explain the problem
- What rules have been broken
- What standard of performance is not being met
- What behaviour is complained of?

(2) State the evidence
- Refer to documents, rules, etc.
- Refer to documented observations of performance or behaviour.
- Give dates, witnesses, etc.

(3) Listen to other side
- Are there any mitigating or extenuating circumstances?
- Is the employee denying a problem exists?
- Is there any dispute over evidence?
- Is any alternative evidence available?

(4) Summarise
- Is there agreement that a problem exists?
- How far apart are the two sides' perceptions of the problem?

(5) Explain what is expected in the future
- Identify specific things to be done or achieved in the future.
- Establish expected standards of performance (by reference to job description, staff appraisal, etc).
- What specific changes need to be made?

(6) Ask what the practice can do to improve the situation
- What resources are needed to improve matters?
- Is training required?
- Are clear practice procedures needed to effect an improvement?

(7) Agree on follow up action
- Who is going to do what?
- When will both parties discuss this again?
- Is the action reasonable and attainable?

---

practice is able to provide (for example, in future the employee
will be expected to lodge all items of service claims with the
FHSA on a specified date; the practice will send the employee on
an FHSA training day to help an understanding of FHSA
procedures and practice); (j) ensuring that staff know what kinds
of behaviour or actions (for example, theft, breach of confidentiality, smoking, etc) will constitute gross misconduct (that is,
justifying summary dismissal); (k) putting in writing any steps
taken that may result in future disciplinary procedures or
dismissal (for example, any informal warnings; any failure to
increase salary after review because of poor performance, etc); (l)
making sure the practice manager (and partners) are trained.
Disciplinary interviews are difficult and those who may have to
conduct them should have the opportunity to practise the skills
involved; (m) reviewing practice procedures regularly; (n)
carrying out investigations as quickly as possible; (o) allowing

---

Dear Mrs Simons

Following our earlier discussion, I would request that you attend a
meeting on Monday 30 April at 10.45 am with Dr Smith and me.
The purpose of the meeting is to discuss the following:

(1) Your failure to notify the practice of your intention to take
    annual leave on 25 and 27 April 1994 contrary to the practice
    policy on notification of annual leave (see staff handbook, page
    3).
(2) The incident on Friday 20 April involving Mr Fry, one of Dr
    Smith's patients, and in particular the alleged argument that
    took place, after which Mr Fry informed Dr Smith of his
    intention of changing doctors.

I shall be inviting Mrs Wilson, senior receptionist, to attend the
meeting to give her version of events on 20 April. As the meeting
may result in disciplinary action, you are encouraged to bring a
friend, colleague, or trade union representative with you to the
meeting. The meeting will be conducted in accordance with the
practice disciplinary procedure (copy attached).

Could you please confirm your availability to attend this meeting.

Yours sincerely

Practice Manager

Figure 14.1 Model letter – invitation to a disciplinary meeting

Dear Mrs Simons

We met on 30 April 1995 at 10.45 am to discuss (*insert specific allegations*). You were represented at the meeting by Mr Deal, UNISON officer. It was agreed at the meeting that the current situation must be rectified and that you would take the following action.

(1) Notify the practice manager of your intention to take annual leave, before booking any holiday.

(2) Also take a full part in the practice rota for holidays and liaise with other reception staff before making any arrangements for leave.

(3) In future desist from arguing with patients at the reception desk. Any complaint from patients should be dealt with in future according to the practice policy on handling complaints. If you have any difficulties with this in the future you should seek the advice or instruction of the practice manager or the partners.

I must warn you that failure to achieve the improvements specified will be likely to lead to further disciplinary action.

The position will be reviewed in 6 months' time and, provided that the necessary improvements have been achieved, no further action will be taken.

I should like to assure you that the practice will make every effort to provide you with any support you might require to achieve the improvements required.

Under the terms of the disciplinary procedure you may appeal against this warning. If you wish to do so you are required to submit your reasons to Dr Curtis, in writing, within 14 days.

Finally, I should be grateful if you would sign the enclosed copy of this formal warning and return it to me as acknowledgment of receipt.

Yours sincerely

Practice Manager

Figure 14.2 Model letter – confirming the outcome of the disciplinary meeting

an employee to be accompanied by a friend, colleague, or trade union representative; (p) allowing a right of appeal. This can give rise to difficulties in small practices. In all cases try to allow for the right of appeal to someone (such as another partner who was not involved in the original hearing). Don't allow a partner or practice manager to become "judge, jury, and prosecutor". Don't (as happened in the case referred to in box 1) have all partners sign disciplinary warnings, which would preclude any right of appeal.

Carrying out a disciplinary interview

Carrying out disciplinary proceedings can be traumatic and stressful. Skill is required, and staff and partners expected to carry out disciplinary interviews should be suitably trained. Remember the purpose of any disciplinary interview is to correct the behaviour of an employee rather than be seen to be imposing sanctions. An interview should pass through various stages with a clear start and finish point. Box 3 gives a suggested procedure for conducting a disciplinary hearing.

Final written warning

Dear Mrs Simons

I write to confirm the points made at our meeting on . . .

As you are aware over the past . . . months you have failed to meet the standards required by the practice in the following respects:

(list areas in which performance or conduct has fallen below the required standards)

As discussed with you we agreed to give you until *(insert date)* to meet the required standard. This means that you will need to take the following action:

(list actions to be taken to meet the required standards of performance)

I must warn you that in view of the previous warnings you have been given, if you fail to achieve the standard of performance/conduct required by the practice by the above date, you will be dismissed.

Under the terms of the disciplinary procedure you may appeal against this final written warning. If you wish to do so you are required to submit your reasons to Dr Curtis, in writing, within 14 days.

Please sign and return the enclosed copy of this final written warning as acknowledgement of receipt.

Your sincerely

Practice Manager

Figure 14.3 Model letter – the final written warning

Putting it all in writing

Any action that is likely to result in some form of disciplinary action should be documented. Remember, employees who may face disciplinary action should be told at every stage of the procedure what is happening. They should be left in no doubt about the nature of the problem; they should be told in advance whether or not a meeting or interview may result in disciplinary action; they should be given the opportunity to prepare their case and to present it with the assistance of a friend, colleague, or trade union representative. They should also be told of any disciplinary decision made and be made fully aware of the action to be taken, the reason for the decision, and the improvement required of them. Figures 14.1, 14.2, and 14.3 are examples of model letters that a practice can use in disciplinary matters.

15 Practice politics – when the knives are out, know the ground rules

Few organisations are completely immune to political infighting. This is as true of general practice as it is of commercial companies or other organisations. Individuals or groups competing for influence or resources, differences of opinion, hidden agendas, and conflicts are features of most organisations. The scope for such political infighting in general practice is often considerable; between partners, partners and staff, manager and staff, and even patients and staff. In small organisations there will always be scope for rivalries, contests, and clashes of personality to develop and, unless confronted, to fester. One management consultant compares organisational policies to the kind of bickering common in every family, and acknowledges that they add a certain colour to human experience. However, they can often be enormously wasteful of time and resources:

> Meetings in companies where politics dominate devote only half an hour to actual business – and 90 minutes to politicking and jostling for position. [Office politics are] often played out of sheer boredom – it's much more fun to take up politics rather than getting on with the job.

Psychologists point out that office politics are often about fear; people are afraid of being rumbled, so playing politics is often a defence mechanism. Though they cannot ever hope to eradicate office politics completely – its roots often run very deep – managers ignore its potency at their peril.

Professor Charles Handy, a leading management theorist, says that "organisations (except for dictatorships and prisons) are inevitably involved in finding compromises, reconciling differences, and living with what is possible rather than what might be ideal". Dealing with organisational politics, therefore, is about managing them rather than trying to eradicate them completely. The best managers are those who are able to reconcile divergent interests at the workplace and to reconcile the differences between individuals and between groups.

Politics is about power

Organisational politics is all about power. Power is the quality that other people perceive an individual to possess, giving that person the ability to influence the action of others. Getting to grips with organisational politics is firstly about finding out which individuals and groups wield power, and how that power is exercised. Next, practice managers need to wield influence themselves, which means having some power. If they haven't enough power of their own they will need the support of others with power (that is, partners).

In any organisation, the sources of individual power that give one person the ability to influence others are:

Physical power – being bigger or stronger than others. This is not used overtly in management but often exercised through a powerful physique, domineering body language, or an authoritative presence – which either unnerves or intimidates others.

Resource power is given to someone who controls access to what others, whether subordinates, peers, or superiors, need (including materials, information, rewards, facilities, time, staff, promotion, or references).

Position power is conferred by a person's position in an organisation (for example, the manager, who is by right allowed to instruct others to carry out tasks).

Expert power is a power vested in someone because of their acknowledged expertise or indispensability.

Personality power – sometimes referred to as "charisma". Managers often wrongly attribute their success or influence to

Examples of negative power

- Withholding information from people who need it
- Distorting information
- Circulating slanderous gossip
- Passing off other people's ideas as their own
- Working to rule
- Reinterpreting the existing rules to ease their own freedom of action
- Empire building
- Fostering a climate of "them" versus "us"
- Forming cliques and in-groups
- Agreeing not to reveal the skeletons in other people's cupboards

this, rather than to their position or resource power in the practice. More often such a power involves a bargaining or personnel skill that enables them to make the most of their other powers, such as resources.

Negative power is the power to stop things happening (usually illegitimately), to distort them, or disrupt them (see box). Organisations that are characterised by high morale and good employee relations are usually not appreciably affected by the exercise of negative power. Conversely, poorly managed organisations are usually characterised by a high degree of negative power being exercised by employees. Remember that an employee who might have low occupational status or occupies no formal leadership or managerial role (perhaps a secretary or a receptionist) may still exert enormous power within an organisation.

Destructive or creative politics

Two types of organisational politics are identifiable. The more destructive negative type of politics involves the scheming and backbiting that are usually aimed at advancing sectional interests rather than being concerned with the best interests of the organisations as a whole. Motives of individuals or groups who indulge in negative politicking might be to:

- Gain more than their fair share of whatever benefits are available
- Block other people's legitimate work plans
- Set people against one another in the workplace
- Seek more and more power for the sake of it
- Pursue personal advancement at the expense of the organisation
- Make themselves immune to criticism
- Prevent other people advancing themselves
- Pursue personal vendettas
- Continually remind people how powerful they are, even if there is nothing to gain in the particular situation.

Unfortunately, in many organisations where there are coffee machines to huddle around or corridors to whisper in there will be jockeying for position for increased power, enhanced status, or more rewards.

The more acceptable face of organisational politics entails a degree of healthy conflict or competition between individuals or groups who all have the best interests of the organisation at heart but disagree about what they are and how they might be achieved.

In his book *Power In and Around Organizations* H Mintzberg outlines a series of political games that are often played out in organisations (see box opposite). He argues that most of these games, when used in moderation, can have a healthy effect on keeping the organisation on its toes. Taken too far, however, they turn the whole organisation into a political cauldron and divert it from its main task.

Getting to grips with the politics

A good practice manager should be able: to identify the individuals or groups that exercise power, in whatever form; to challenge the exercise of power when it is disruptive and harmful to the harmonious running of the practice; and, if necessary, to acquire more power for themselves (or maximise the power that they already have). Strategies for achieving these objectives might include getting control of resources, gathering information, maintaining expertise (remember that managers who lose touch with the expertise that is the basis of the operation they manage

---

Mintzberg's political games in organisations

Games to resist authority:

● The insurgency games – to sabotage the intentions of superiors;

Games to counter resistance:

● The counterinsurgency games – more rules, regulations, and punishments;

Games to build power bases:

● The sponsorship game – hitching oneself to a useful superior, a star;

● The alliance game – finding useful colleagues;

● The empire game – building coalitions of subordinates;

● The budgeting game – getting control of resources;

● The expertise game – flaunting and feigning expertise;

● The lording game – flaunting one's authority;

Games to defeat rivals:

● The line versus staff game – between units or functions;

Games to change the organisation:

● The strategic candidates game – informing on an opponent;

● The young Turks game – enclaves of key rebels.

---

are in danger of losing credibility in the eyes of their colleagues), or doing favours, etc. Other useful ways of mobilising personal power are:

● Identifying all the powerful and influential people at the workplace

● Collaborating with others where interests are sufficiently similar

● Lobbying – getting support from others on particular issues

● Avoiding antagonising people who might add to the political chicanery going on around them

● Doing favours (by providing resources, support, and information) and expecting reciprocation

● Listening in to the practice grapevine and developing an unofficial network of staff so as to gain access to valuable information and support which you might not otherwise get in your position as manager

- Negotiating with individuals to win their support in offering your support in return
- Winning people over to your side by persuading them of the positive gains that can be made by supporting you or the practice
- When an individual is resistant to your advances, arranging for that individual to be approached by one or more people he or she respects who happen to be your supporters (for example, one of the partners)
- Volunteering to take on tasks and projects that give you control of more resources
- Letting it be seen that you use what power you have in an open, responsible, and public spirited fashion – and not for self aggrandisement or personal gain
- Exposing the political chicanery of others when such behaviour undermines the smooth running of the practice.

General practice can be a fertile ground for the office politician. Though not able to eradicate politics entirely, a manager can neutralise the effects of negative politicking – which is harmful to the wellbeing of the practice – by a combination of personal influence and exercising power reasonably themselves. Day to day conflicts that arise in all organisations can, by good management, be turned into either fruitful competition or purposeful argument, which will be to the benefit of the practice.

Further reading
Mintzberg H. *Power In and Around Organizations*. New York: Prentice Hall, 1983.
Handy C. *Understanding Organisations*. London: Penguin 1987.

16 Stressed staff

It is estimated that every working day nearly 270 000 people take time off because of a stress related illness, including heart disease, depression, and hypertension. This is 23 times more than the time lost through industrial action. The time lost to the NHS and the costs associated with lost production and efficiency amount to billions of pounds each year. Rapid organisational change, economic recession, and unemployment mean that workplace pressures are mounting almost daily. It is not – as legend would have us believe – the high powered middle aged executives who are the main victims of occupational stress. According to Peter Warr at the applied psychology unit at the University of Sheffield, "research has repeatedly indicated that the lowest mental health, in terms of greater anxiety and depression and lower active involvement in life, is found among workers at the bottom of the organisation, not among the supposedly overstressed executives".

In general practice, the increasing demands and pressures caused by recent NHS changes mean that practice staff are increasingly suffering higher levels of stress.

Absenteeism caused by stress poses practical problems for running any general practice. It is costly in terms of providing temporary cover, administering any practice sick pay scheme, and increased overtime costs. Additionally, it puts pressure on other staff and on administrative time because rota arrangements have to be changed. It also disrupts work flows and can affect staff morale and motivation generally.

Causes of stress at work

Although stress has been recognised for many years as causing personal difficulties, employers have only recently begun to recognise the problem. Liz Sayce of MIND believes that part of the problem is cultural: "people don't find stress an easy thing to talk about. Employees are worried that they will be seen as less competent if they admit to difficulties, and employers don't know how to cope with someone with a problem." To help staff deal with stress GPs need to be aware of the causes (see box).

One particular source of stress at work arises from the employer and employee relationship itself. The way people are managed has an effect on their mental, emotional, and professional wellbeing. A "good" boss can help to motivate staff to perform to their maximum efficiency. A "bad" boss on the other hand can literally make someone ill. For example an unpredictable boss can cause staff to spend more time worrying about the boss's mood than they spend on their work. Staff prefer to live in the knowledge that a certain action will produce a certain outcome, that good work will merit praise and mistakes will earn a reprimand.

Low self esteem at work is another source of stress. Eroding a person's sense of self esteem – for whatever reason – should always be avoided. Never, for example humiliate someone in front of colleagues; make unwarranted or unjust criticisms; ridicule or disparage an employee; deny an employee recognition; or take credit, or allow others to take credit, for work an employee has done.

Creating win/lose situations can also cause stress. Always winning at the expense of a member of staff can lead to a sense of submissiveness and low self esteem. The results may be (a) hostility and distrust, (b) stifled sensitivity and empathy, (c) constant wrangling and conflict, and (d) reduced levels of creativity and flow of new ideas.

Preventing stress

People respond to stress in different ways and the ability to cope with stress at work will vary from person to person. There is no definitive checklist of symptoms. Generally, the symptoms include physiological signs (such as insomnia, stomach pains, headaches), emotional signs (such as tiredness, depression, irritability), and behavioural signs (such as increased absenteeism,

Most common sources of stress at work

Intrinsic to job

- Too much or too little work
- Poor physcial working conditions
- Time pressures, etc

Role in organisation

- Role conflict or ambiguity
- Responsibility for people
- No participation in decision-making, etc

Career development

- Overpromotion
- Underpromotion
- Lack of job security
- Thwarted ambition, etc

Individual

- Personality
    - Tolerance for ambiguity
    - Ability to cope with change
- Motivation

Relationships within organisation

- Poor relationships with boss
- Poor relationships with colleagues and subordinates
- Difficulties in delegating responsibility, etc

Organisation interface with outside

- Company *v* family demands
- Company *v* own interests, etc

Being in the organisation

- Lack of effective consultation
- Restrictions on behaviour
- Office politics, etc

Source: Cooper, M. *Stress and Pressures Within Organisations*. Management Decision 1975; **13**, No 5: 292-303.

Stress management courses

Courses are often intended as a preventative measure for stress related problems, rather than as treatment for existing ones. The idea is to teach employees greater control over aspects of their lives that are subject to stress.

Stress management includes:

- Muscle relaxation
- Diet and exercise
- Biofeedback
- Meditation
- Time management
- Assertiveness

inactivity, declining job performance). Other signs include indecisiveness, lack of concentration, and loss of libido.

The earlier that damaging stress symptoms are identified, the easier it is to take steps to reduce it. This may be through (a) more support and personal encouragement, (b) temporary reduction in work pressures, (c) stress management courses (see box), or (d) improved communications and counselling (some large employers, for example, operate a stress counselling service for employees). According to MIND's Liz Sayce "as well as providing counselling, it is important to provide preventative measures to decide what is causing the stress to avoid a vicious circle which can culminate in people having to leave their jobs, which adds to their problems."

An increasing interest in stress at work has recently been shown by employers. According to legal experts this is because of the greater potential of employees taking legal action. A recent UK case involved an employee who claimed that he had had a nervous breakdown because of stress caused by a reduction in numbers in his work group, and it resulted in a successful negligence claim against his employer. According to Jill Earnshaw, lecturer in law at the school of management at the University of Manchester Institute of Science and Technology, the danger of UK employers being sued by their employees for causing them stress is a timebomb waiting to go off.

17 Sexual harassment at work

There is nothing new about sexual harrassment at work; thousands of women have put up with it for years. In recent years, however, the issue has been the topic of widespread public debate. Evidence suggests that sexual harassment is a problem in virtually every workplace. Surveys in Britain, the US, and Europe support the view that a substantial proportion of women have been sexually harassed at some time during their working lives. In general practice, apart from anecdotal evidence, there has been an increase in the number of cases being referred to industrial tribunals.

What is sexual harassment?

Sexual harassment is a particularly antisocial and unacceptable form of behaviour that, until quite recently, went largely unrecognised. A European Commission code of practice on the subject defines sexual harassment as "unwanted conduct of a sexual nature or other conduct based on sex affecting the dignity of women and men at work" (see box overleaf).

Introducing a new NHS agreement on harassment in March 1992, Virginia Bottomley said "many do not know how to cope with harassment. Some eventually leave the workforce, and this is a tragedy both for the individual and the health service. Every employee, male as well as female, has the right to respect and dignity at work." Many misconceptions are held about what

107

European Commission code of practice on sexual harassment

The code recommends that employers should:

- Issue a policy statement, which expressly states that all employees have a right to be treated with dignity, that sexual harassment at work will not be permitted or condoned, and that employees have a right to complain about it, should it occur

- Communicate effectively to all employees the organisation's policy to ensure that employees are treated with dignity

- Give managers (including supervisors) a particular duty to ensure that sexual harassment does not occur in work areas for which they are responsible and provide specialist training in the subject

If harassment has occurred the code says that:

- Employers should designate someone to provide advice and assistance to employees subjected to sexual harassment

- A formal complaints procedure should specify to whom the employee should bring a complaint, and it should also provide an alternative if, in the particular circumstances, the normal grievance procedure may not be suitable

- Violations of the organisation's policy should be treated as a disciplinary offence and the disciplinary rules should make clear what is regarded as inappropriate behaviour at work

---

constitutes sexual harassment (see box opposite). Its essential characteristic is that it is unwanted by and unwelcome to the recipient, which distinguishes it from acts of mutual flattery, flirtation, or harmless romantic behaviour. It can take many forms and an employer's failure to recognise the unwelcome and unwanted aspects of a harasser's behaviour is often what leads to harassment being trivialised. It usually involves one or more of the following:

- Insensitive jokes or pranks carried too far
- Displays of pornographic pictures
- Lewd comments about physical appearance
- Requests for sexual favours or bantering about aspects of a person's private life
- Explicit sexual violence, unwelcome sexual advances, or propositions

---

Common myths about sexual harassment

- It is part of everyday working life and the natural order of things
- It is nothing more than lighthearted fun which can do no harm, and need not be taken too seriously
- It is a figment of the victim's imagination
- It is easily coped with
- It is usually an attempt to initiate sexual relations
- Harassment is a "personal" matter, of no concern to an employer or partner
- Women find it flattering and use it to manipulate men
- It is of no legal consequence

- Sexist or patronising behaviour
- Continued suggestions for social activity outside the workplace after it has been made clear that such suggestions are unwelcome.

Consequences of sexual harassment

The consequences of sexual harassment at work should be considered on three levels.

The employee

Evidence shows that sexual harassment extracts a high price from its victims. It can subject employees to fear, stress, and anxiety that put great strain on personal and family life. It can lead to illness, increased absenteeism, lack of commitment and motivation, poor performance, and even resignation. All these have a direct effect on an organisation's effectiveness.

The employer

Employers should never underestimate the damage, tension, and conflict in the workplace that sexual harassment creates. The result is not just poor morale but higher labour turnover and staff conflict. The results are difficult to measure but will eventually show in the performance of the organisation.

109

Legal consequences

Until recently, the legal consequences of sexual harassment were uncertain. The Sex Discrimination Act, 1975 does not specifically cover harassment. It does, however, provide that people discriminate against a women if "on the grounds of sex they treat her less favourably than they treat or would treat a man," resulting in the complainant suffering a detriment – that is dismissal, denial of job benefits, or "any other detriment."

The courts have interpreted this as including within the definition conditions in the work environment. In a leading case in 1986 the judge said "sexual harassment is particularly degrading and is not acceptable, and it must have been the intention of Parliament to include such treatment within the sex discrimination legislation." When sexual harassment is proved, the remedies include a declaration that harassment has occurred, an award of compensation (including a separate award for injured feelings), and a recommendation that the employer take action to "obviate or reduce the adverse effects on the complainant."

The seriousness with which the law treats sexual harassment is reflected in the level of compensation awarded. Since 1986, the number of claims brought to tribunals have steadily increased. Latest figures show that since 1986 the tribunals have decided 97 sexual harassment cases, 63 of which were successful. Compensation awards have ranged from £109 to £7 000. In cases settled before tribunals awards of up to £15 000 have been made. Separate awards for injury to feelings have ranged from £100 to £8 925. Recent changes in British law have resulted in the statutory limits previously applied to tribunal awards in sexual harassment cases being removed. Employers who permit acts of sexual harassment may also be held to be in breach of contract of employment, entitling employees to resign and treat themselves as constructively dismissed.

How to handle allegations of sexual harassment

Sexual harassment is a sensitive and serious matter and should be dealt with promptly and sympathetically. Dealing with such allegations needs full investigation. Managers should avoid condoning any allegation, making light of the situation, or jumping to conclusions. They should allow the people involved to describe the situation as they see it.

If action is required, first establish whether the person concerned would be competent and willing to tell the alleged harasser that he or she will not tolerate such behaviour. Alternatively, the person may choose to write the harasser a letter containing the exact date(s) when and place(s) where the alleged harassment took place. Those who find themsleves the victim of harassments, are often least able to protect themselves. They may be young, lacking in interpersonal skills, or shy and inhibited. In such circumstances the employer or manager should confront the harasser. Managers should remember that sexual harassment is not only insulting and demeaning to the recipient but is also potentially actionable under law and could land the employer with a bill of compensation amounting to several thousand pounds.

It is important that procedures for dealing with sexual harassment are included in the practice grievance and disciplinary procedure. At the same time, however, it must be recognised that in many cases the victim may be dissuaded from coming forward and that, by its nature, harassment may make normal channels of handling grievance complaints difficult to use. Employees subject to harassment should therefore be entitled to seek advice, support, and counselling in confidence, without any obligation to take a complaint further. Only when the complaint cannot be resolved informally should the matter be dealt with under formal complaints procedures.

Sexual harassment in any form is unacceptable and degrading. All employers large and small should be prepared to deal with outbreaks. All the evidence suggests that harassment is a widespread phenomenon and is attributable to outmoded attitudes and stereotyping of men and women. It is also associated with abuse of power in the working environment.

Tribunals are now taking a more robust approach to claims of sexual harassment. The possibility of having to make large compensation payments to victims should ensure that all employees take the necessary steps to protect their workplaces from incidents of sexual harassment.

18 Staff commitment

In most workplaces – general practice is no exception – there are enormous, untapped reserves of talent and enthusiasm. Despite stereotypes to the contrary, people are keen to work to their fullest potential, be more effective, and contribute to the success of the organisation that employs them. Opinion surveys on attitudes to work show overwhelmingly that people feel uncomfortable when not working to full capacity, while nearly three quarters feel that they could be more effective. It appears that the Protestant work ethic is alive and well.

Encouraging greater enthusiasm and releasing this untapped potential means that managers need to engender in their staff a sense of involvement and commitment to the aims and objectives of the practice. Radical changes in the NHS and general practice are making a new vision (based on commitment) more and more vital to success.

What is commitment?

Employee commitment describes the loyalty and attachment that people feel for their work and the organisation that employs them. It involves people giving their all at work and is often encapsulated in comments such as:

- I feel a sense of satisfaction when I do my job well
- I like to look back on a day's work well done
- I think of ways of doing my job more effectively
- I live, eat, and sleep my present job
- I would stay over and finish a job even if I'm not paid
- I take pride in doing my job as well as I can.

Commitment also involves accepting change, cooperating with others in the implementation of change, and a willingness to try something new. Staff with high loyalty feel committed to the practice. They give their best and feel good when giving their effort because it is seen as being in the best interests of the practice.

Commitment is not the same as involvement or compliance. Involvement usually describes the process of allowing staff to be involved in decisions about working arrangements and how their work is done. Compliance means employees observing rules and carrying out instructions. Commitment on the other hand involves a belief in, and acceptance of, the goals and values of the practice as well as a commitment to the job. Commitment is always voluntary and personal and, unlike duty and obligation, cannot be imposed. Unlike involvement, it cannot be initiated by others and, because it is given voluntarily it can also be withdrawn.

What are the benefits of increasing commitment?

It is assumed that increasing employee commitment will result in improvement in peformance and effort. In their book *Creating a Committed Workforce* Martin and Nicholls distinguish between three levels of commitment: (1) commitment to work in general, which is likely to result in a conscientious and self motivated approach to work, regular attendance, minimum supervision, and a high level of effort; (2) commitment to a specific job, which results in a higher level of effort as well as self esteem and is associated with ambition and career progression; and (3) commitment to the organisation, which results in reduced absenteeism and turnover and in the attainment of organisational goals and objectives.

Japanese management has led the way in devising strategies to involve employees and to engender commitment. It has been shown that Japanese, as well as American, companies that adopt a progressive view in their management of people are both more profitable and faster growing. Whereas many British managers are often characterised as defensive, authoritarian, conservative, and poor at consultation, others are fast recognising the importance of

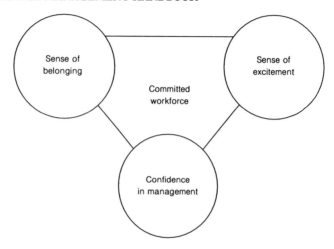

Figure 18.1 The three main pillars for creating commitment

providing open, honest, and regular information to employees, as well as fully involving them at the workplace.

Components of commitment

Martin and Nicholls state that there are three main pillars for creating commitment.

A sense of belonging makes an important contribution to commitment. It is one of the most powerful forces that bind people together in communities, families, clubs, etc. Practice managers could create a sense of belonging by keeping staff informed, involving them in decisions, and allowing them to share in the success of the practice – thus making sure that they feel valued (see box opposite).

Sense of excitement about one's work increases motivation. People need to feel pride in their work, to be trusted, and to be accountable for their efforts. Pride, trust, and accountability create a strong incentive for individuals to perform well, which reinforces commitment and loyalty.

Confidence in management – A lack of confidence in management often leads to a sense of cynicism and alienation. To win a person's commitment, managers must display trust, competence, and dedication. Moreover, they must exert authority and maintain a high professional standard.

Practical steps to making staff feel valued

Make subordinates feel valued by

- Regularly monitoring their work
- Sharing an interest in whatever they hold important
- Creating an atmosphere of approval and cooperation
- Ensuring that every subordinate understands the importance of his or her contribution to the team's objectives
- Ensuring that every subordinate understands the function of the practice

Provide scope for development by

- Setting targets for all staff
- Providing on and off the job training
- Arranging any necessary internal and external contacts
- Using staff to train others in the specialist skills they may have
- Restructuring or grouping tasks to use staff skills to the fullest.

Recognise achievements by

- Praising and communicating individual successes
- Reporting regularly on the practice team's progress
- Holding regular meetings to monitor and to give advice on an individual's progress towards targets
- Explaining the practice results and achievements.

Provide challenge by

- Setting and communicating practice aims and objectives
- Providing scope for individuals to take greater responsibility
- Training thoroughly
- Encouraging ideas and, when practical, allowing employees responsibility for implementing them.

Policies for creating commitment

Martin and Nicholls suggest that involvement and commitment do not just happen. Managers need to actively create a climate in which staff feel a sense of belonging, a sense of excitement, and a sense of confidence in their managers. The evidence shows that

115

Policies for creating a committed workforce

How to produce a sense of belonging

- Inform people by: team briefing
  open disclosure
  simple language and example

- Involve people by: single status conditions
  consultation
  social as well as work events

- Share success by: bonuses
  performance related pay

How to produce a sense of excitement in the job

- Create pride by: responsibility for quality
  direct identification with results
  comparison with competitors

- Create trust by: peer group control
  removal of demarcation

- Create accountability for results by: pushing decision making
  down the line
  challenging assignments
  creating quality circles

How to produce confidence in management

- Exert authority by: maintaining standards and objectives

- Show dedication by: attention to commitment
  reducing management overheads
  seeking productivity through people

- Display competence by establishing: objectives
  new management initiatives
  professional standards

the effort of building a committed workforce is certainly worthwhile. According to the authors, by designing policies around these three pillars, managers can successfully build a committed and well motivated workforce (see box). These policies give a useful guide to the variety of management techniques and practices that can be used in building commitment.

The meaning of employee commitment is undoubtedly a complex matter. Much of what is written on the subject is basic common sense. Experience, however, shows that building a committed workforce does have positive results in terms of performance, effort, and effectiveness. A high level of employee commitment implies a willingness to work for the practice's benefit. However, obtaining employee commitment depends on reciprocal commitment by the practice. Staff can be expected to perform well if:

- They are trained and are clear about how to do their jobs
- Their role has been clearly defined in consultation with them
- Their achievements are valued and recognised
- Their loyalty is translated into active commitment.

To some extent all practice policies will affect employee commitment. For this reason managers need to review existing policies and practices and ensure that staff are fully involved and consulted on proposed changes.

Further reading
Martin P, Nicholls J. *Creating a committed workforce.* Institute of Personnel Management, 1989.

19 Managing conflict at work

Conflict between people is inevitable. It arises in every organisation and is the normal byproduct of people trying to work together. In general practice differences inevitably arise between partners and staff, between patients and staff, and between partners themselves.

Some forms of conflict can seriously damage the practice as well as staff morale. Other forms of conflict, if handled correctly, can be constructive and yield benefits for the practice. When conflict is dealt with openly, staff are stimulated to seek solutions, to resolve differences, and to be more searching and creative. Unfortunately, on too many occasions conflict is not confronted openly, but is ignored. The task of the GP or practice manager is to tackle conflict and to manage it constructively (see box).

Managing conflict entails:

- Anticipating and preventing destructive conflict
- Limiting the number of outbreaks
- Dealing with it before it gets out of control
- Encouraging constructive differences and benefiting from such differences

---

Symptoms of conflict

There are many symptoms of conflict at work; it does not always manifest itself in such obvious ways as arguments and raised voices. Sometimes conflict will reveal itself in low morale, poor performance, high absenteeism, and greater levels of stress. Interpersonal conflict will often deteriorate over time into icy formality and into situations in which every problem becomes polarised around people and personalities. Frustration and anger generated by conflict is often directed at those higher in authority, such as partners or practice managers. Even if as an experienced GP or manager you recognise the symptoms of conflict in the practice, you will have to find ways to deal with it. You therefore have to seek out the underlying causes of the conflict.

Common causes of conflict at work

Because people have different perceptions, some individuals in a practice will often not be aware of any conflict around them, whereas others may be only too aware of the longrunning hostility and disagreement between, say, the practice nurse and one of the partners.

A particular event, such as the introduction of a new computer system, may be seen by some as a challenge and by others as a threat. People's perceptions are influenced by social conditioning, personal history, and vested interests. Before setting out to tackle conflict it is always good policy to check what other people's perceptions are of the situation.

Conflicts often arise over work related issues (see box), such as the persistent lateness or absence of an employee. The situation will deteriorate when other staff perceive that the issue is not being addressed. In tackling such issues it is important to get to the source of the problem. Does the conflict arise from the work situation, is it personal, or caused by domestic or emotional problems? Has the issue been a longrunning and persistent source of conflict? Conflict may also arise where individuals (or groups) disagree about important issues. When individuals are in competition for something that only one of them can have, such as the secretary's time, conflict will also inevitably arise.

Sometimes the symptoms of conflict will result in an individual lashing out and blaming evryone around them for a problem. In these circumstances it is important to focus on the specific cause

119

Issues that cause conflict

- How best to achieve common objectives – for example, to maximise practice income or optimum level of patient care
- Work priorities – for example, improving the quality of reception service or improving the decoration in the waiting room
- Style of management – for example, flexibility and pragmatism or rigid adherence to rules and regulations
- Who has the right to decide certain issues – for example, the practice nurse or the practice manager?

of the problem and to clarify the critical issues. Diagnosing a problem that is causing conflict also helps to identify other "stake holders" and to anticipate other potential problems.

Not all conflict is bad

Encouraging the expression of differences will often be beneficial to the practice. Managing constructive conflict can, however, be difficult and requires considerable interpersonal skills – and reserves of tolerance. If handled badly the situation could destabilise the practice team and produce polarisation and result in further destructive conflicts. For example, conflict may:

- Bring a problem out into the open
- Stimulate different solutions to a problem
- Reveal where people stand on an issue
- Allow the practice team to assert itself
- Encourage creativity and "brainstorming"
- Provoke a "catharsis" by releasing interpersonal conflicts of long standing.

Dealing with conflict

People react differently to conflict. An individual may choose to ignore it in the hope it will all blow over. Others will confront it head on by threatening some form of sanction, such as disciplinary action. Broadly, there are three ways of reacting to conflict, avoiding it, diffusing it, or facing up to it.

(1) Avoiding conflict – This usually involves:

- Denying it exists
- Sidestepping the issue
- Not raising the issue
- Postponing it until another time
- Avoiding the person with whom you're in conflict.

(2) Diffusing the conflict may involve:

- Smoothing things over
- Dealing only with minor points, not major ones
- Yielding to another's point of view
- Saying you'll come back to the problem.

(3) Facing up to the conflict – aggressively or assertively

You can face up to conflict either

Aggressively by:

- Using status or threatening sanctions
- Refusing to concede that the other person has a valid point
- Belittling the other point of view
- Interrupting the other person
- Arguing dogmatically
- Exaggerating your case

Assertively by

- Searching for a mutually acceptable solution
- Understanding the other person's point of view
- Being open about your objective
- Stating your case clearly
- Developing the other person's ideas
- Summarising to check understanding or agreement.

The important thing to remember in attempting to resolve conflict is to keep talking and to keep the issue in focus by not allowing yourself to be sidetracked. Dealing with disagreements and conflicts requires skill. To influence people and situations a practice manager must be seen as being positive and constructive. Being positive and constructive in the face of resistance—and often open hostility—means being assertive. Being assertive involves:

- Stating clearly that you disagree
- Expressing doubts and criticism constructively

121

Twenty ways to prevent conflict

1 Hold regular staff or practice meetings
2 Get GPs support for the active management of staff
3 Take firm but fair action over any lack of agreement on work issues
4 Consult staff before making decisions that affect their work
5 Avoid hasty decisions that you may regret later
6 Avoid criticising staff in front of others
7 Don't make personal attacks on people behind their backs (and discourage others from doing this)
8 Ensure that the practice has good selection procedures
9 Keep job descriptions and contracts up to date
10 Avoid making assumptions about how people feel; check with them first
11 Always have a grievance procedure
12 Don't avoid tackling individuals whose conduct is unsatisfactory
13 Counsel staff whose competence or conduct is in question
14 Provide for regular staff appraisal or performance review
15 Don't allow small cliques to form in the practice team
16 In resolving disagreements don't leave one or both parties with bad feelings
17 Don't back people into corners from which they can't escape
18 Remind staff that the success of the practice depends on teamwork
19 Praise people for being helpful and supportive
20 Don't sidestep issues that may result in future disagreements

- Changing your opinion in the light of new information
- Giving reasons for your disagreement
- Stating exactly what you disagree with
- Recognising other people's point of view
- Distinguishing between fact and opinion
- Using "I" statements such as "I think . . . I want . . . I feel"
- Giving helpful feedback.

Preventative measures

The best way to manage conflict is to prevent it arising in the first place. Although disagreements are bound to arise from time to time, the checklist in the box provides useful ideas for preventing conflict in the practice.

20 Dealing with a problem drinker

The financial cost of alcohol misuse in society as a whole runs into hundreds of millions of pounds. Evidence shows that drinking can lead to domestic, financial, and health difficulties. It can often result in the loss of a job, divorce, and serious long term ill health. It is estimated that for every problem drinker up to four other people are affected by the drinker's behaviour. Research shows that the number of problem drinkers in Britain is as high as 1 in 10 of the total adult population. Most experts agree that the figure is increasing. The cost of alcohol misuse is difficult to assess but a recent estimate suggests that the nation's bill for dealing with alcohol misuse could be in excess of £2 billion – taking into account the cost to industry and the NHS, running national agencies, and dealing with traffic accidents and crime.

Employers are at the front line

The problem of alcohol misuse is widespread. The fact that up to 75% of problem drinkers are in full time employment means that most employers will at some stage be affected in terms of increased absenteeism, accidents and reduced work performance. As Norman Willis, former general secretary of the Trades Union Congress (TUC) acknowledged, "problem drinking is a tragedy of growing proportions. Contrary to popular belief, the majority of problem drinkers are not down and outs but are to be found in employment, often tolerated by colleagues and management until their condition worsens into a state of chronic incompetence

123

whereupon they leave because of deteriorating health or are simply dismissed."

Alcohol misuse has in fact become British industry's costliest drug problem. According to the Institute of Personnel Management (IPM) three quarters of employers say they have a problem with alcohol misuse, and 5% of staff admit their performance has been affected by drinking in the past year. Absenteeism among heavy drinkers is likely to be twice as high as for other workers. Industry loses up to 14 million days a year through absenteeism caused by drinking—four times the number lost through strikes. The total cost to industry has been estimated at £1·7 billion in sickness absence and premature deaths.

Common problems associated with alcohol misuse at work include absenteeism, lateness, impaired performance, and antisocial behaviour. Employees are a practice's greatest asset but an employee with an alcohol problem is likely to lower overall productivity and morale, decrease the quality of work, worsen employee relations, and may even put patient relations at risk. Some employers respond to an alcohol problem by dismissing the employee concerned. It is estimated that dismissing an employee and hiring and training a new person can cost three times as much as helping an existing employee to deal with the problem. It is generally more cost effective for an employer to encourage treatment rather than continue to sustain the cost of continuing poor performance, dismissal, early retirement, or an accident.

Alcohol misuse policies

With increasing recognition of alcoholism as an illness, alcohol policies at the workplace have become an important employment issue in recent years. Both the Health and Safety Executive and the Department of Health recommend that an alcohol policy should be a written extension of an employer's health and safety policy required under the 1974 Health and Safety at Work Act. Policies should also tie in with the practice's existing disciplinary procedures (although because employing organisations differ, there can be no blueprint or model policy). Any policy should be tailored to the size and specific needs of a practice. There are, however, some key issues which should be considered when drawing up a policy.

Prevention

Even if there is not an immediate problem, it makes sense to do all you can to prevent one happening in the future. Prevention is often less costly than cure. Health care premises are an ideal place to promote an awareness of drink related problems and to help those with an alcohol problem. Information on the problems of alcohol misuse and leaflets on sensible drinking should be made available to staff as well as patients. Information on the practice alcohol policy should be included in the staff handbook. When staff come forward with a problem then a policy should ensure that they are treated fairly and sympathetically.

Recognising a problem

The practice may already have a system of monitoring work performance. Although changes in behaviour may not be obvious, eventually employees who are misusing alcohol will begin to show the signs and these will become observable by others around them. Some behaviour patterns to be considered are set out in the box.

What should you do about it?

Any policy on alcohol misuse should aim to help a problem drinker before their job is put in jeopardy. In many cases employers and colleagues have turned a blind eye to the problem in the hope that it may disappear or the person concerned leave. A practice policy should, however, work in tandem with the practice disciplinary procedures and if necessary can be used to persuade the employee concerned to accept a referral for treatment. Matters related to alcohol misuse should be treated confidentially. The policy should cover, too, such things as job security, sickness absence and benefits, and time off for treatment. If time off is needed for counselling or treatment it should, when possible, be granted. Employers should also:

- Encourage employees to seek help voluntarily
- Provide advice and any other type of help needed
- Offer an opportunity for help where work has deteriorated
- Give the same protection and employment rights that you

125

Recognising the problem of alcohol abuse

Absenteeism

- Pattern of Monday to Friday absences
- Excessive lateness
- Excessive use of sick leave
- Unauthorised leave
- Unexplained absence
- Improbable excuses for missed time
- Other people telephoning with reasons for absence

Accident rate

- Accident and safety related issues at work and home

Work performance

- Impairment of good performance
- Tasks require greater effort and more time
- Inaccuracy
- Failure to meet deadlines
- Improbable excuses for poor work performance
- Lack of reliability and predictability
- Long coffee and tea breaks and frequent visits to the cloakroom
- Difficulty with or complaints from patients

Reporting to work under the influence

- Coming to work in an obviously inebriated condition
- Smelling of alcohol
- Hand tremors
- Increasingly unkempt appearance or lack of personal hygiene

Poor employee relations at work

- Overreaction to real or imagined criticism
- Unreasonable resentments
- Irritability
- Complaints from other members of staff
- Borrowing money from colleagues

would to other employees who have problems related to ill health

- Treat employees sympathetically if they relapse and give them another chance if they take advice and undergo treatment.

Interview guidelines

- Hold the interview in private and communicate with others on a "need to know" basis only
- Make sure that the facts are reliable. Confront the employee with facts only and then the practice policy and consequences
- Listen carefully to the explanation given and document it
- Limit the discussion to job performance issues such as attendance, behaviour, attitude, and relationship with other staff and partners
- Acknowledge the employee's positive contributions both past and present
- Consult partners, if appropriate, both before and after the interview
- Make sure all records are held securely and remain confidential
- Make it clear to the employee that help will be offered and in what form, and encourage the employee to use it
- Ensure that the employee understands the consequences of repeated poor work performance
- Explain what action will be taken, ensure that the employee understands this, and attempt to seek a positive commitment from the employee
- Set a date for a review meeting
- If necessary follow normal disciplinary procedures

What not *to do*

- Jump to conclusions
- Make accusations
- Assume facts
- Moralise or preach to the employee
- Be unfair or inconsistent
- Get involved in a verbal battle in an attempt to prove right or wrong

If you become concerned about an employee's possible misuse of alcohol you need to handle the matter very delicately. At some stage this will probably involve interviewing the person concerned, when you should follow certain guidelines (see box).

Implementing a policy

The aim of a practice policy on alcohol misuse should be to reduce the possibility of losing good employees at the same time as ensuring that health and safety standards are maintained. As a manager you should accept responsibility for helping those whose drinking habits are affecting work performance or those who are worried about their drinking habits. The policy should be communicated to staff. The staff handbook is probably the best way of ensuring that all staff are aware of the policy. Once in place the policy should be monitored and regularly reviewed. Records should be kept and a watching eye should be kept on the pattern of absence in the practice.

Alcohol policy and the law

In their advisory handbook, *Discipline at Work*, ACAS indicate that an alcohol policy should identify employees suffering from alcohol misuse and encourage them to seek help. The aim of such a policy should be to create a climate in which dismissals are not necessary. If employers do resort to dismissal, however, the existence of an alcohol policy will usually put them in a better position to defend claims of unfair dismissal. If a dismissal is on the basis of an employee's capability to do his job or related to his conduct then employers who follow the policy should have established a reasonable view of an employee's medical condition after allowing a reasonable period of treatment. So dismissal in such circumstances would probably be fair. Employers are obliged to make it clear to employees in their disciplinary procedure what, if any, drinking offences (for example, drunken behaviour) will be categorised as misconduct. Tribunals do not expect an employer to support and tolerate a drinking problem indefinitely. If an employer has tried to help a problem drinker over a considerable period of time it may not be considered unfair to dismiss the employee if he or she continues drinking. There comes a time when an employer must say "enough is enough".

Further reading

Discipline at Work. Advisory, Conciliatory and Arbitration Services (ACAS)

21 Managing change

The 1990 contract forced GPs to look closely at the working arrangements in their practices. The performance related nature of the contract means that having the right people in the right place doing the right thing is a major determinant of success in general practice. Fundholding and a greater emphasis on "consumer relations" and quality of service have meant practices having to review working practices and policies.

With turbulent times ahead, few practices can afford to remain static. Change is inevitable and it has to be managed but as Machiavelli once observed "there is nothing more difficult to carry out, nor more doubtful of success, nor more dangerous to handle than to introduce a new order of things".

In practices where staff are well informed, motivated, and committed managing change should present few difficulties if there is a high degree of trust between GPs and staff. Staff will readily adjust and embrace changes which are seen to be in the interests of the practice. In practices characterised by poor management, low morale and trust, and poor communications, problems will inevitably arise where changes to working practices are anticipated. The box illustrates some typical problems associated with change. In tackling such problems GPs need to understand: (a) why resistance to change occurs, (b) how to deal with resistance, and (c) the possible legal consequences.

Why resistance to change occurs

Without venturing too deeply into the realms of human psychology, many common causes of resistance can be found.

130

Examples of problems associated with change

- After the retirement of the senior partner, the incoming partner soon became concerned about the irregular hours being worked by reception staff. As the practice was planning to become fundholding, the partner decided to introduce more regular working practices. One member of staff refused to accept any changes to her established pattern of work

- A fundholding practice recently carried out a quality audit. One of the proposed changes was the introduction of uniforms for practice staff. It was agreed that the uniform would be paid for an maintained by the practice. The design and colour was to be agreed by staff at the practice meeting. One member of staff indicated her refusal to wear any uniform

- A practice recently introduced a no-smoking policy prohibiting smoking throughout the practice premises. One member of staff claimed she was addicted and insisted on being given time and a place to allow her the occasional cigarette. She threatened to resign

- A receptionist was informed that the partners intend to close the branch surgery, where she has worked for 10 years, as it was no longer viable. It was proposed that she transfer to the main surgery three miles away, but she refused for domestic reasons

These are rarely due to simple cause and effect and are usually a complex mix of historical, factual, and emotional issues that are not easy to disentangle. The most common causes of resistance to change are:

- Fear of the unknown
- Lack of information
- Misinformation
- Historical factors
- Threat to skills and competence
- Threat to status
- Threat to power base
- No perceived benefits
- Climate of low trust
- Poor working relationships
- Fear of failure
- Fear of looking stupid

- Reluctance to experiment
- Being custom bound
- Reluctance to let go.

Some situations are easier to deal with than others. For example, resistance caused by a lack of information is easier to overcome than having to deal with the legacy of many years of neglect of employee relationships and low trust relationships with staff.

When resistance to changes occurs then the best policy is to identify the causes and address the underlying problems. The most important factor in influencing people to change their views is to involve them in the process.

Tackling resistance

Changes – large and small – will always provide some degree of resistance. The status quo is a powerful stimulus, and the "better the devil we know" mentality of some staff means that GPs need to devise appropriate strategies to meet such resistance.

Strategies for dealing with resistance

Negotiation If self interest is an element in a person's resistance then the offer of some incentive in return for concessions or agreement may be appropriate.

Education If there is a misunderstanding or lack of trust or a situation where staff are fearful of change, then the best strategy is to communicate the reason for the changes and the likely benefits for the practice as well as the individuals. When the majority are committed and willing to go along with change they will undoubtedly influence any potential dissenter.

Participation Where perceptions of proposed changes result in resistance, then the best approach would be to involve those resisting change in its design and implementation. For example, where staff uniforms were proposed in one practice, potential resisters were invited to participate in the design and choice of the uniform. All research shows that participation leads to higher levels of commitment.

Force and support When staff resistance stems from the fear that they will not be able to cope with changes, another approach is to force the change through and then give maximum support and encouragement to staff in coming to terms with changed circumstances. The argument in favour of this strategy is similar to that in support of legislation that forces people to change their ways – for example, to wear seatbelts or not to discriminate on grounds of sex or race. This approach gambles that people will eventually come to terms with the changes or recognise that the changes were not too bad after all.

The legal aspects of change

When proposed changes involve greater flexibility, revised hours of work, or measures that affect other conditions of employment, GPs are faced with two legal considerations; do the proposed changes interfere with or break staff contracts? To what extent will the practice be open to a legal challenge in an industrial tribunal?

A contract of employment can only be varied lawfully by mutual consent. An exception would be when the contract contains a flexibility clause, which allows changes to be made. Either by imposing a change in the terms, or by introducing a new contract, a GP could be liable for breach of contract or unfair dismissal. Employees who refuse to accept a change but continue to work under amended terms for any length of time may have implicitly accepted the change. An industrial tribunal would decide a case on the basis of whether the GP had acted fairly and reasonably. In judging the fairness of an employer's decision the courts have said that the reorganisation of a business, together with an employee's refusal to accept a modified contract, constitutes a fair reason to justify the dismissal. A GP could avoid a tribunal if he can show that the proposed changes are aimed at the efficient running or the financial well being of the practice.

As well as acting fairly, an employer must be seen to act reasonably. The standard of reasonableness expected of employers involves taking the following action: (a) trying to obtain agreement to changes, (b) explaining why changes are required, (c) exploring alternative courses of action, (d) discussing consequences of non-acceptance, and (e) listening to employees' concerns and trying to address them.

In the long run good management practices will prevent claims and avoid potential pitfalls. GPs who keep staff informed and who have earned their respect are more likely to find that staff will adjust to reasonable and necessary changes in working practices. It is poor management, inadequate communications, and distrust that leads to a reluctance and fear of change – and ultimately to possible legal action.

22 Handling patients' complaints

Any practice manager will tell you that one of the most common complaints from patients is that they are unable to see the doctor of their choice at a time convenient to themselves. Unmet expectations, frustrations, delays, abrupt or rude reception staff (often unintentionally), are all regular causes of complaints from patients – sometimes to the FHSA. As patient expectations have risen so have their complaints.

Though many GPs would argue that it is they who need protecting from the rising tide of apparently irrational and sometimes unfounded complaints coming from patients, practices can no longer afford to be complacent. Like it or not, today's general practice is conducted in a completely different environment and there are clear financial consequences in ignoring any patient dissatisfaction – patients may simply go elsewhere. One practice manager has told of how one patient wrote to her informing her of the whole family's intention to change to another practice after an insensitive remark made by a receptionist during a telephone conversation.

Lessons can be learnt from industry and commerce where "customer care" programmes have been around for some time. In business, survey evidence shows clearly how damaging poor customer relations can be (see box 1). The analogy between patients and customers is, of course, a crude one. Dealing with a difficult patient in a health centre is very different from dealing with a customer in a commercial environment. Yet practices can learn from the world of commerce. Complaints always need to be

---

Box 1 – Learning from the business world – surveys of businesses show:

- For every customer who complains, 25 others remain silent
- Over 90% of unhappy customers will never purchase the organisation's products or services again
- The average aggrieved customer will tell 8-16 other people
- Is is five times more expensive for an organisation to attract a new customer than to keep an old one
- Once the complainants have had a grievance remedied, up to 95% will continue to make purchases
- Quality is the "silent" salesperson

---

properly handled by the practice team. Improving practice organisation, making sure that staff are sensitive towards patients' needs and anxieties, and introducing quality awareness

---

Box 2 – Common myths about patient complaints

- "If patients don't complain we are obviously doing a good job"
  Not so. Most unhappy patients don't complain
- "Losing one patient won't damage the practice"
  But dissatisfied patients are likely to tell others
- "If we make it hard to complain, we won't be bothered by petty problems"
  Not so; it is better to let patients know that complaints will be dealt with by the practice. Remember that complaining patients are sometimes the practice's most caring patients
- "We can always attract new patients"
  This is not always possible
- "Even if we satisfy the complaining patients, they will not come back"
  Not so; patients who complain and are helped will show more loyalty than those who never complain
- "Patients who complain are just trouble makers"
  Not so; complaining involves time and inconvenience and can also be an expensive procedure for patients

---

and complaint handling techniques will promote the practice's image by enhancing patient satisfaction and in turn patient loyalty.

Handling patient complaints

Practices should aim for a policy that ensures that good patient services prevail throughout the practice and make sure that it also covers patient visits and calls. In handling complaints staff should be encouraged to:

- Show interest by indicating to the complainant that you are listening
- Empathise; put yourself in the patient's place. They may be distressed, anxious about a relative, or in pain. Imagine how you would feel in the same position

---

Box 3 – How to deal with telephone complaints

- Create a positive image by being friendly, courteous, helpful, and businesslike towards patients
- Identify yourself immediately; do not leave the caller in a position where they have to guess to whom they are speaking. Answer calls promptly
- Keep a pen and paper handy to make notes and take messages
- Take accurate messages (for example, date, time, name of patient, phone number, reasons for call, next action, etc)
- Use a practice message form. Use appropriate language; avoid jargon
- Return calls promptly
- Suggest a time for a return call
- Avoid interruptions
- Do not do all the talking; give the caller time to think and respond
- Speak calmly and be sympathetic to complaining callers. Do not cover up with excuses. Thank them, investigate, and call them back
- If you must put a call on hold, give the caller the choice of being called back instead (and agree a time)
- If you transfer a call, tell callers to whom they will be talking

---

- Gather all the information available and do not jump to conclusions. Let the patient say his or her piece
- Be tactful. For example, ask if there is a problem with the prescription rather than saying "You have forgotten to take the tablets"
- Restate the complaint – to show that you listened and to make sure there are no misunderstandings
- If there is a problem, admit it – and apologise for any inconvenience caused
- Find out what the patient wants to see happen, rather than asking brusquely "What do you expect me to do about it?"

Some dos and don'ts

Professionals in the specialty of customer relations stress the

---

Box 4 – Dos and don'ts

Do
- Explore all the possible ways of resolving the problem
- Be positive by showing what you can do and not what you can't
- Concentrate on correcting the problem, don't dwell on what went wrong
- Be on the patient's side, don't oppose him or her (for example, say "Let's see what we can do")
- If the complainant is angered let him or her let off steam

Don't
- Abandon the patient while the problem is being checked out
- Take the complaint personally
- Be defensive or argue with the patient. If a problem exists, agree
- Cause further disappointment by promising something that can't be delivered
- Assign blame to others
- Say no without an explanation
- Lose your sense of humour

---

importance of some basic dos and don'ts when handling complaints (see box 4).

In every case, complaints from patients should be followed up. Staff should be encouraged to contact the complainant by telephone or in writing to ensure that the problem has been resolved and that the patient is satisfied with the result. Recurring

Box 5 – How to be a good listener

Practice policy on handling complaints should follow the 10 commandments for good listening:

- Stop talking. You can't listen if you are talking, and if you are talking you are not learning anything

- Put speakers at ease. Encourage them. Try putting their feelings into words to show you understand – for example, "I am sorry to hear my decision has upset you. I do appreciate what you are telling me. Tell me what we can do about the problem"

- Show that you want to listen. Give your full attention and listen carefully. Nod and make encouraging remarks: "Yes, I see what you mean"

- Remove any possible distractions. Shut the door, turn off the radio, do not doodle or walk about

- Put yourself in the speaker's place. See his/her point of view: "Why did they say that? What would I have said if I had been in that position?"

- Be patient. Allow plenty of time for listening. Do not interrupt and do not keep looking at your watch

- Control your emotions. If you get emotional you will not hear properly. You will get the wrong message

- Go easy on argument and criticism. Ask questions to draw out the speaker: "Why did you say that? Is that what you really feel? What facts do you have to support that statement?"

- Do not argue or attack their views. If you put speakers on the defensive they may clam up or become emotional

- Ask questions. They encourage the speaker and show that you are listening. Also ask questions to develop the topic

- Summarise review, and reflect. Summarise what you think speakers have said and repeat their words. This will help them remember

---

Box 6 – Practice protocol on patient complaints

- Information to patients on the practice complaints procedures; this should be referred to in the practice leaflet

- A clearly defined procedure detailing the timescales in which the complainant should be seen and an explanation given as well as procedures for carrying out investigation, etc.

- A log book of complaints detailing time and date of complaint, who and how it was dealt with and follow up and outcomes

- The training of staff to deal with patient complaints; this should be incorporated into the practice induction programme for new staff

---

complaints should be fully discussed at practice meetings – they may point to larger problems – and setting up a log of complaints might be a good idea. Practice policy should never be criticised in front of patients; comments and criticisms should be brought to the practice meeting.

Brush up your listening skills

Dealing with complaints requires patience and a great deal of listening. Most of the literature and communication emphasises the need to improve listening techniques, and your practice complaints policy should take account of this. So if you do not know where to start handling complaints, brush up on your listening (see box 5).

A practice protocol on dealing with patient complaints should be drawn up, which includes the points in box 6.

23 Practice meetings – how to survive them

Meetings, meetings, and more meetings. They can be the curse of a GPs working life – meetings with partners, staff, nurses, health visitors, FHSA officers, the Friday meeting with drug representatives – all take up valuable time in a partner's busy schedule. Meetings can be notoriously unproductive, unstructured, and boring. Alternatively, they are criticised as being a hindrance to decision making, bogged down in trivia, or for providing a platform for the practice windbag. One disgruntled practice manager recently reported that she spent more time discussing arrangements for staff holidays at practice meetings than any other subject.

Practice meetings are, however, important and should be open, productive, and cooperative. Moreover they should be enjoyable. People should go to them because they want to, not because they have to. They should feel that they personally, as well as the practice, will benefit from them and they should come away from them feeling that their time has been used constructively. Meetings involving staff are particularly important. They play a vital role in ensuring job satisfaction and involvement. Never being told what is going on in the practice, or what is being planned, or never being involved in decision making leads to a sense of isolation and is a certain recipe for disaffection and poor relations with staff.

Though there are many good reasons for holding practice meetings, there are just as many bad reasons for having them.

Meetings should not be held:

Points to consider

Before the meeting

- What is the purpose of the meeting - is it necessary?
- Who is to be present?
- Where and when is it to be held?
- Have you read all the relevant papers?
- Have you read the minutes or action list of the previous meeting to see what business needs following up?
- Is the agenda planned, and have priorities been set?
- Have you decided how you are to deal with difficult issues or individuals?
- Does everybody know what his or her contribution should be? (indicate names against topics on the agenda)

At the meeting

- Start (and finish) on time
- Call the meeting to order
- Open meetings formally—state the purpose of the meeting
- Don't smile benignly at late comers
- Preserve order and act in a businesslike way
- Review the agenda or action list
- Remain neutral during discussion
- Prevent irrelevant and repetitious discussion
- Summarise and reach conclusions to ensure that things get done

After the meeting

- Circulate minutes or action list
- Follow up and coordinate to see that action is taken

- Out of habit
- To avoid seeing patients
- To avoid responsibility
- As a means to a free drug lunch
- For partners or staff to flex their muscles
- To avoid work.

Surviving practice meetings

Problem	Symptoms	Suggested action
Poor leadership	Time "hogged" by one or two people Members not allowed a proper hearing. Chair talked too much. Non-agenda items discussed.	Suggest changing or rotating chair. Suggest chair reads Citrine's *ABC of chairmanship* (NCLC Publishing Society Ltd, £5).
Lack of purpose or objectives	No minutes or action list from previous meeting Overlong agenda. No priorities.	Summarise main purpose and objectives of meeting before starting. Shorten the agenda, divide contents under appropriate headings.
Timekeeping	Members arrive late. Not starting on time. Overruns	Make sure start and finish times are clear. Start on time. Do not wait for latecomers. Stick to the agenda.
Disruptions	Telephone interruptions.	Make sure meeting takes place outside busy times for the surgery. Switch on the answering machine. Ensure that members have relevant papers before meeting starts. Encourage chair to assert his or her authority.
Poor start/ finish	Objectives or purpose not clearly defined. Meeting ends on "negative" note. Feeling tht time has been wasted.	Spell out objectives and purpose at the start. End on a positive note. Encourage sense of accomplishment. Summarise action at the end.
Lack of focus and direction	No decision reached on important topics. Meeting wanders off course.	Summarise issues to be discussed and decision to be reached. Refocus the discussions. Remind members of purpose of meeting. Have a five minute break and restart.
Conflict	Disagreements over decisions reached. General release of hostility or anger.	As long as individuals stick to the subject and time, let them say their piece. Do not allow personal abuse.
Hidden agenda	Members allowed to "grind their own axes". Scoring points off other members. Not addressing the real issues.	Ignore the hidden agenda and move the meeting on, or expose and confront it.
Domineering individuals	Discussions dominated by the practice "knowall" or experts who like the sound of their own voices.	Ensure maximum participation so that the conforming power of the group reduces the influence of deviant or difficult individuals.

143

Practice meetings should not be held if they are simply a means of rubber stamping decisions already made. This will only leave staff feeling duped.

To be effective, meetings should be as democratic as possible. Furthermore, they need to be managed. In most cases the major cause of ineffective meetings is poor leadership or chairmanship.

Successful practice meetings are planned meetings, for which consideration has been given to the best time of day (outside surgery hours) and the best location (away from telephones and other interruptions). If you are to be responsible for organising or chairing a practice meeting, consider the points in the box on page 142.

The purpose of a practice meeting may be to pass on information, solve a particular problem, or make decisions. Alternatively, it may have been called to evaluate a proposal or share the experience of everyone in the practice over a particular incident or occurrence. It may provide an opportunity to air practice grievances. The overall aim of the meeting may be to encourage team spirit in the practice. Whatever the purpose it will be effective only if everyone participates.

People operating in groups act differently from the way they do as individuals. The psychology of people in groups has been a subject of considerable research – and many personality types have been identified. Apart from the moaners, the knowalls, the conspirators, and the obsessives ("types" who will be familiar to followers of the television medical comedy series *A Very Peculiar Practice*), there are those who remain silent throughout the meeting and make no contribution at all. This allows the practice talker to take over and derail the meeting. It requires the skill of the chairman or group leader to encourage the otherwise silent members to join in (following the Spanish Inquisition technique of pouncing on people and demanding their views is not a recommended way of getting the best out of anybody at the meeting).

Beware the hidden agenda

Some practice meetings are characterised by hostility and disagreement among staff and partners. Such hostility often reveals a hidden agenda (see the box on page 143). Hidden agendas come in many forms: a dispute between partners; conflict between the practice manager and staff over hours worked or conditions in the practice; the receptionist trying to discredit the practice nurse; or a staff member riding a favourite hobby horse. Whatever the cause, hidden agendas can destroy a practice meeting if ignored. A grudge between two people can subvert any discussion no matter what the subject, bringing the meeting to a grinding and embarrassing halt. As long as the grudge persists the members will go from meeting to meeting turning the debate into personal battles. The language of the hidden agenda can also be revealing. For example, "The suggestion I made last time on reorganising the reception area, was ignored" may mean "I am not being appreciated by the practice manager".

Dealing with personal agendas can be difficult. They can either be ignored or exposed. To ignore them may mean that all future practice meetings are flawed. Alternatively, the hidden agenda can be exposed and discussed at the meeting. If a hidden agenda reveals a dispute between two or more partners then it may be more appropriate to discuss at a specially convened partners' meeting.

Plan the agenda

Meetings can be enormously time consuming. In planning meetings make sure that the agenda is properly thought out. A time limit needs to be set for the whole agenda as well as individual items. When possible, individuals should be encouraged to think ahead about subjects on the agenda and come to the meeting prepared – this will save time. As "any other business" can mean a further opportunity for individuals to ride their hobby horses, it may be better to seek the consent of the meeting or alternatively agree in advance what items will be included under this heading.

Effective practice meetings should be a means of ensuring that the practice runs smoothly and allow staff and partners to act together as a team. They should be rewarding both to the individual and to the practice (in terms of time and money). The sense of achievement reached at practice meetings should reap rich rewards in terms of commitment, motivation, and guiding the practice forward. But, remember, next time you convene a practice meeting, ask two questions: (a) is the meeting really necessary or could the time be used better? and (b) is the meeting the best way of achieving your declared objectives?

24 Avoiding the pitfalls of partnerships

A doctor going into general practice is entering not only a business arrangement but usually a partnership for life (not unlike marriage some would say!). As the basis for a long term career commitment it is better to sort out areas of potential difficulty before disputes arise rather than afterwards. Fundholding and the 1990 GP contract have in many cases increased the scope for potential partnership disagreements. A written partnership agreement is essential. An incoming partner should, however, always check on the existence of any previous partnership agreement. Legally, incoming partners could be bound by an existing agreement, and any restrictions it contains, if they are aware of its existence and if they have explicitly or implicitly acted on the terms of such an agreement.

Partnership agreements

In partnership agreements the topics which commonly cause problems are as follows:

Restrictive covenant

The sale of goodwill in general practice is unlawful (see box). A practice can, nevertheless, protect its established custom and popularity by including a restrictive covenant in a partnership deed. Without such a covenant an outgoing partner can set up in the area without restriction, causing a reduction

---

Sale of goodwill

The sale of goodwill in general practice is unlawful under the 1977 NHS Act. The Act gives powers to the Medical Practices Committee (MPC) to certify whether or not a proposed partnership transaction – such as the sale or valuation of practice premises – involves a sale of goodwill. A deemed sale of goodwill exists where "the consideration for the sale is substantially in excess of the consideration which might reasonably have been expected if the premises had not previously been used for the purposes of a medical practice."

The MPC can be contacted at 9th Floor, Euston Tower, 286 Euston Road, London NW1 3DN Telephone: 0171 388 6471

---

in the number of patients and financial loss to the practice. Any restraint, however, must be reasonable in terms of both duration and geography; it should apply equally to all the partners and should be defined solely in terms of the partnership patients. It should not attempt to restrict an outgoing partner in any capacity other than a GP. A court is unlikely to uphold any restriction it considers to be unreasonable. Moreover the Medical Practices Committee (MPC) may consider an unreasonable restraint as evidence of sale of goodwill. It is always better to have a limited restraint that can be enforced rather than an extensive one that cannot.

Workload

The 1990 contract explicitly linked GPs' pay to performance. It is not suprising therefore that the reported number of disputes over workload have increased. An incoming partner may be faced with taking over the greater share of the practice workload, including an onerous on call commitment. Such a situation inevitably leads to discontent and conflict. When a partner's share of workload is greatly out of proportion to his share of the profits, a sale of goodwill may again be implied. Partnerships need to decide how to deal with such outside interests as private practice and medical appointments (such as clinical assistantships). It would be advisable to include a clause stating that partners are obliged to devote themselves whole time to the practice and that they are not to engage in any other business without the consent of

147

the other partners. If a partner's commitment is limited this will, of course, affect the basic practice allowance, depending on whether the commitment is full time, three quarter time, half time, or a jobshare arrangement.

Income

Problems arise when an agreement deals with who gets what but without defining what constitutes practice income. Partners should specify which NHS appointments count as personal income and which should be shared. It is often better for all fees and earnings from whatever source to form part of the partnership income. There is no hard and fast rule, however, and the main thing is to get agreement on the issues that may cause problems. Topics that should be clarified include:

- Seniority payments
- Postgraduate education allowance
- Legacies
- Night visit fees
- Private practice
- Medical appointments outside the practice.

Profit sharing arrangements

Arrangements for profit sharing must be agreed and specified in the agreement, along with the starting share of incoming partners and the agreed steps to parity, which should normally take three years. Longer periods could be deemed to be an implied sale of goodwill. For a doctor to be treated as a partner, he or she must be a principal and the arrangements for sharing the partnership profits must comply with the availability options set out in the regulations. Profit sharing arrangements should not be tied to any list size conditions. For example, a GP recently objected to her senior partner including in the partnership agreement a clause guaranteeing equal shares after three years, provided that the combined lists of the patients was in excess of 4500. Given the geographical area, it was unlikely that such a condition could ever be fulfilled.

Leave arrangements

Leave arrangements of partners often prove troublesome. An inordinate amount of time can be consumed working out practice arrangements for leave. Ultimately a degree of compromise is required. The partnership agreement should specify the amount of leave, any arrangements for locum cover for absent partners, and whether locum costs are borne by the partnership or the absent partner. It is also advisable to include a restriction on the number of partners who can take holiday leave at the same time. A formal holiday rota may be appropriate to overcome problems of popular periods such as school holidays. Leave arrangements should cover not only holidays and sickness absence but also study leave, sabbaticals, maternity, and parental leave.

Maternity arrangements

"A potential minefield" was the response of one GP when asked about his practice's arrangements for maternity leave. Because of legal developments both in the UK and Europe, maternity provisions need to be kept under review. Currently a female partner who is pregnant should be treated in the same way as a comparable male colleague. This means maternity leave and benefits must be the same as sickness leave and benefits for a male partner. A female partner should not suffer financially as a consequence of her pregnancy. To grant maternity benefit and leave on less advantageous terms than those for sick leave could be construed as sex discrimination. Although there are no statutory provisions covering partnership and maternity arrangements, there are General Medical Services Committee (GMSC) recommendations (see box).

Maternity leave recommendations of the GMSC

- A minimum of 13 weeks' absence for maternity leave
- Arrangements should cover the actual workload of the partners, not just hours of availability
- A maximum period of leave should be specififed
- Arrangements for maternity leave should not affect entitlement to holiday and sickness leave
- Adoption leave provision should be included, if necessary
- Paternity leave, if agreed, should be specified

149

Junior partners

Cases of exploitation of junior partners abound. The independent contractor status of general practice means that legal options to prevent such exploitation are limited. Also employment protection rights do not apply to partners. Advice to junior partners should include: (a) find out all you can about the practice before starting; (b) check, if possible, the details of previous partnership arrangements with the outgoing partner; (c) take advice from a solicitor and accountant independent of the partnership interests; (d) seek guidance and advice from a knowledgeable source such as the BMA regional office, the local medical committee, or if appropriate the Family Health Service Authority; (e) check whether an old agreement exists (remember you could be bound to this if you implicitly accept the terms – see above); (f) check that the draft agreement covers all the items included in the checklist on page 152; (g) make sure that the period of mutual assessment is reasonable – that is up to six months; (h) make sure that the time taken to reach parity and steps taken on the way are clearly defined; (i) are the arrangements for profit sharing free from any conditions about list size? (j) do not sign anything until you have read it and if necessary taken advice; (k) has the date been fixed by which partnership terms are to be considered and have you received a letter of intent confirming the partnership and identifying its principal terms?

Leaving the partnership

Under the 1890 Partnership Act a partner cannot be expelled unless the partnership deed covers such a possibility. It is vital therefore for an agreement to specify: (a) any provision for dissolution; (b) the conditions under which partners may retire, either voluntarily or involuntarily; (c) the required period of notice; (d) arrangements for the shares of any outgoing partner to revert to the remaining partners. A comprehensive list of dos and don'ts should be included, with provision for expulsion for failure to observe them (for example, lengthy incapacity, bankruptcy, removal or suspension from the medical register, or gross breaches of the agreement).

Capital

Capital assets of the partnership include not only the practice

150

premises but also practice equipment, stocks of drugs, fittings, and furniture. Incoming partners usually take a share in the assets and working capital of the practice. Problems usually arise over the question of practice premises. Clearly a major concern of an incoming partner will be security, the arrangements for buying into the practice, and the valuation of practice property. The question of timing varies, but the stage of a partner reaching parity usually provides the best time to buy her or his share of the practice premises. Buying in immediately or in stages aligned to steps to parity is often – depending on the area – not a feasible option given the capital outlay and sums involved. In any event, it is important that partnership accounts show clearly the individual partners' holdings in the assets or capital of the firm and that the partners understand how these have been computed. Where there is an obligation to purchase the premises, the basis of valuation for both incoming and departing partners must be agreed. There should also be an agreed period of notice to be given to the remaining partners by an outgoing partner (or his estate) in the event of the outgoing partner (or his estate) wishing to acquire the premises for their own use. Whatever method of valuation is used goodwill must not be included.

Resolving disputes

Several horror stories have been reported recently in which partnership disputes have resulted in the near bankruptcy of partners. Scant coverage is given to the costs involved in these cases, in terms of personal stress and family anxiety. These factors often outweigh the monetary aspects. In one recent case a partner faced increasing demands from his former four partners, who wanted to get him out of the practice area following a protracted partnership split up. The partners issued a writ alleging that a restrictive convenant contained in an earlier agreement was still enforceable. Despite being advised by his solicitor that the writ had little chance of succeeding, the experience put immense psychological and financial pressure on the sole partner, which affected both his work and his family life.

To avoid the traumas and costs involved, partners should consider as mandatory a provision for arbitration in the agreement. Differences of opinion which could lead to more fundamental differences can be resolved within the partnership often with the assistance and advice of mediators appointed by the

Checklist of points to cover in partnership agreements

- Nature of the business, and names of partners
- Duration of the partnership, and date of commencement
- Capital assets
- Premises
- Partners' liabilities
- Partnership income
- Workload distribution
- Expenses
- Bank account
- Accounting, tax (including a continuation election), and super-annuation
- Profit sharing basis
- Private work
- Hospital appointments
- Decision-making arrangements
- Gifts and legacies
- Who signs cheques
- Medical defence
- Leave arrangements (holiday, study, sabbatical, maternity, parental, etc)
- Retirement
- Expulsion
- Restrictive covenant
- Departure of partner (share of capital, valuation of capital, etc)
- Arbitration

BMA or the local medical committee. The first requirement of resolving any difficulty is to keep talking. Communication is the lifeblood of any partnership, and simply ignoring a problem or brushing aside differences is a certain recipe for future problems.

25 Implementing a no smoking policy

The public generally, and health care professionals in particular, are increasingly intolerant of smoking in public places as well as the workplace. Yet in some health service premises the issue of staff smoking remains a problem. General practice is at the vanguard of good practice aimed at preventing ill health, particularly with regard to the effects of smoking, and all practices should address the issue of smoking at work as a matter of priority.

Health dangers

No one working in health care needs to be reminded of the fact that, although a minority activity in the UK, tobacco smoking is still the largest single cause of preventable ill health and death in the country. It is known to be associated with cancer of the lung, coronary artery disease (heart attack), and a wide range of cardiovascular disorders including strokes.

There is also mounting scientific evidence of health risks associated with involuntary or passive smoking (sometimes called environmental tobacco smoking or ETS). According to a recent report from the Imperial Cancer Research Campaign and the Cancer Research Campaign the risks from passive smoking are greater than those from "any other indoor manmade pollutant released into the environment". The report was endorsed by more than 50 organisations including the BMA, the Royal College of Physicians, the Health Education Authority, and the Royal College of Nursing.

Opinion surveys show quite clearly that the large majority of people in the country (90%) believe that more action should be taken to reduce tobacco smoking and restrict smoking in public places. When asked to identify places from where smoking should be excluded by far the most common proposed are hospitals and health service premises.

Although there is no legal ban on smoking there is a growing awareness among experts and employers that a legal challenge in the UK associated with the effects of smoking (including passive smoking) at the workplace is imminent. An early indication of legal attitudes was revealed recently in a case where the Social Security Commission decided that an asthma sufferer's exposure to tobacco smoking at work had caused her to suffer an industrial injury and that she was therefore able to claim state benefit. Although this case did not set a precedent, employers are becoming increasingly

---

Key points in relation to smoking at work and the law

- Employers are under both criminal and common law duties to protect employees' health and ensure a safe working environment

- It would be very difficult for any GP or practice manager to argue that they did not know the health hazards associated with smoking and passive smoking

- Employers have a higher duty of care to individuals such as asthmatics, who are likely to be more affected by smoking at work

- It is advisable to include a term in the contract of employment of new staff whereby they agree to abide by the practice no smoking policy

- A practice is free to hire only non-smokers

- The imposition of a smoking ban on an individual could be in breach of contract and entitle the individual to resign and claim constructive dismissal, but only if the situation was handled insensitively and without proper consultation

- The enforcement of a no smoking policy should be treated in the same way as any other health and safety regulation in the practice

- The result of a breach of these regulations should be spelt out in the practice disciplinary procedure and the staff handbook

- Enforcement difficulties should be overcome by counselling

---

concerned. In the United States a woman was awarded $30 000 for "permanent sensitisation to inhalation of secondhand smoke" arising from sharing a workplace with smokers.

A smoke free work environment

Pressure to establish a smoke free working environment is also coming from political sources. For example the Labour party is committed to introducing legislation enshrining the right to a smoke free working environment. The Institute of Personnel Management in a recent publication notes that the right of smokers and non-smokers has "become one of the hottest topical problems" for managers.

Most practices will have a policy, either written or tacitly accepted, on smoking at work. Those that have not should see that it is given priority. The matter, however needs to be approached with great sensitivity. One practice manager in the north west recently encountered difficulties in introducing a general ban on smoking. On the Monday after the introduction of the ban two recalcitrant reception staff were seen at the start of morning surgery on the steps of the health centre indulging in their perilous pleasure.

There has been a recent deluge of advice and guidance on smoking at work (see Further reading). Practice managers need to be aware of this advice and to frame practice policy in the light of "best practice". There is no single approach to implementing a no smoking policy. A unilateral restriction may lead to resentment and conflict among smokers and non-smokers. In enforcing a no smoking policy a better approach might proceed along the following lines:

- Always remember that many smokers are genuinely addicted, and your policy should take this into account
- Be positive—don't be against smokers but for clean air
- Work out an agreed plan between partners, managers, and practice staff (communication is vital and in the best interests of employee relations)
- Explore all policy options, and canvas opinions from smokers and non-smokers. Agree a phasing in period and a deadline when the practice will become smoke free
- Allow, if necessary, a trial period
- Monitor and review progress

- Gain support and commitment from everyone, including the partners
- Provide as much help for smokers as possible. Involve the partners and, if the practice runs a no smoking clinic, suggest that staff attend.

In formulating a practice policy, the following options might be considered:

- Segregating smokers from non-smokers
- Improving ventilation
- Restricting smokers to a certain area or separate room in the practice
- Banning smoking altogether
- Restricting smoking to certain times of the day, preferably away from surgery times.

Once a policy has been agreed it should be set out and communicated to everyone in the practice. The following checklist might also be included:

- A preamble giving the reasons for the policy
- A statement that the policy applies to staff and partners
- Information about any designated smoking areas
- How the practice will deal with non-observance of smoking restrictions (for example, counselling, disciplinary procedures)
- Restrictions applying to visitors and patients.

Essentially a policy should guarantee the rights of non-smokers to breathe smoke-free air but when possible it should also take account of the needs of smokers. Clearly in general practice a ban on smoking would be more desirable as health premises should be setting the public at large a good example in the light of the overwhelming evidence of the dangers associated with smoking.

Further reading

Health and Employment. Advisory, Conciliatory and Arbitration Service (ACAS) advisory booklet No 15.
Guidelines for a Policy. ASH, 5–11 Mortimer Street, London W1N 7RH.
Smoking Policies at Work and *Passive Smoking at Work.* Health Education Authority, Hamilton House, Mabledon Place, London WC1H 9TX.
Smoking at Work: an IPM Guide. Institute of Personnel Management, IPM House, Camp Road, Wimbledon SW19 4UX.

26 Using the telephone effectively

Although an indispensable means of communication and a great time saver, the telephone can be a curse. The inappropriate use of the telephone is expensive, time wasting, and can produce a poor image of the practice to patients and the wider public. Surveys show that 90% of managers in industry spend over one hour a day on the phone. Over 40% spend two hours or more a day on the phone.

Like it or not, today's general practice is conducted in a competitive environment; impressions are therefore important. In every conversation people remember the impression they get from a phone call. Devoting time to improving the telephone technique of practice staff (as well as partners) can pay dividends. Setting aside practice time to train staff in telephone techniques can help to increase patient satisfaction and help boost the image of the practice.

Telephone behaviour

Despite the obvious advantages of using the telephone as a communication tool there are disadvantages too:

- It is more difficult to establish rapport on the telephone
- By telephoning you are more likely to intrude at an inconvenient time, without necessarily realising it
- Without physical cues, such as body language, there is a greater scope for misunderstanding

157

- During a telephone conversation you are more likely to be distracted and let your attention wander (caller does not see you signing letters, doing the crossword, or reading this month's *Practice Manager*)
- People remember more of what they see than what they hear.

Prepare a staff training programme

Staff training programmes on improved telephone techniques are increasingly popular and should be part of a continuing programme of improving quality of services to patients. A practice training session should cover the following subjects: creating a positive image, answering the telephone, planning calls, dos and don'ts, answerphones, and telephone complaints.

Creating a positive image

Impressions depend entirely on what is heard. Remember the old adage that you never get a second chance to create a good first impression. When using the telephone you should always:

- Be courteous (use expressions like "please," "thank you," "you're welcome," "are you able to hold for a moment")
- Be businesslike (a businesslike approach keeps the conversation from meandering)
- Be brief
- Establish your identity
- Keep your writing hand free
- Use a notepad or message sheet
- Speak distinctly.

Answering the phone

- Answer promptly (within three rings if possible)
- Take notes (see Figure 26.1)
- Be friendly
- Concentrate (avoid talking to others or anything that distracts).

Calls should be planned – When planning telephone calls you should:

- Identify what you need to say during a telephone call so that all information (files, records, and other documentation) is at hand and clearly visible
- Identify the main points in the documentation to which you mean to refer (use a highlighter pen)

A list of dos and don'ts

Do
- Give the name of the practice followed by "good morning" or "good afternoon" to callers
- Answer promptly
- Remain calm, polite, and helpful
- Be brief: calls are charged by distance and length of time
- Speak normally but a little more slowly
- Tell callers frequently that you are trying to connect them
- Thank callers for their time
- Remember to call back if you promised to do so
- Always have a pad of special telephone message forms (see fig. 26.1) and a pen
- Read messages back to callers as a check before they ring off

Don't
- Just answer "hello"
- Ignore a ringing telephone; the caller may be in a call box
- Lose your temper, even if callers do
- Encourage callers to chat idly
- Shout
- Let callers wait in complete silence; they may think that they have been cut off
- Bang the receiver down
- Take a message and let the caller go without asking the name, address, or telephone number
- Rely on your memory: write the message down

- Plan the order of the message: it will be easier for people to understand quickly if it is in a logical order
- If the call is to obtain information have a list of questions you wish to ask so that you can get the answers accurately and quickly during the call
- If you have to go through a switchboard note extension numbers and whether names are correct.

Telephone answering machines

Telephone answering machines still produce terror in otherwise rational and articulate people (a reaction similar to stage fright). Greeted by a recorded message many people still prefer to hang up immediately before leaving any message. Yet the use of answering machines both at home and work is growing rapidly.

159

Recording a message

- State your name and number
- Apologise that no one is available to answer the call in person
- Give an invitation to record after the tone
- Make a statement to the effect that the call will be returned as soon as possible
- If appropriate, give a number where the doctors can be contacted in an emergency.

Leaving a message

- give your name, position, and telephone number

TELEPHONE MESSAGE

TO . . . .

FROM . . . .

of . . . .

Tel no   . . . . (HOME)

. . . . (WORK) Extension . . . .

TELEPHONED		PLEASE RING	
CALLED TO SEE YOU		WILL CALL AGAIN	
WANTS TO SEE YOU		URGENT	

MESSAGE

. . . .

. . . .

. . . .

DATE . . . . TIME . . . .

RECEIVED BY . . . .

Figure 26.1 Sample message form

Points for handling telephone complaints

- Identify yourself to the caller
- Offer to help: if you need to direct the patient elsewhere, explain why
- Show sympathy and understanding; put yourself in the caller's place
- Don't jump to conclusions; no matter how familiar the complaint, gather all the information about the matter
- Be tactful and ask questions
- Show you're listening by restating the situation
- Don't assign blame to others or pass the buck
- Don't behave defensively or argue with patients
- Be positive; stress what you can do for the patient not what you can't; focus on the future not the past
- Let the complainant let off steam before trying to resolve the position
- Don't take a complaint personally
- Contact the patient again to make sure that problem has been resolved and to make sure the patient is satisfied with the result

---

- the date and time that you are calling
- the nature of the call (very briefly)
- a time when you could be called back or when you intend to call back.

Handling telephone complaints

Given some of the disadvantages mentioned above, complaints from patients made over the telephone have to be dealt with using considerable skill and tact.

27 Going to an industrial tribunal – when managing becomes a trial

Case history

For Dr John Waite, partner at the Langdale Medical Centre, the three days in January spent ensconced on the 6th floor of Alexandra House in Manchester was an experience he is unlikely to forget.

Alexandra House, a drab 1960s development, is home of the Regional Office of the Industrial Tribunals. The sixth and seventh floor accommodation has recently been renovated and extended to cope with the increased number of cases being heard by tribunals. Dr Waite was appearing, along with his four GP colleagues and the practice manager, to respond to an application brought by Mrs Jones, the former practice receptionist, who was alleging "constructive dismissal".

To most GPs the prospect of appearing before an industrial tribunal is remote. Few will have experienced the trauma, the costs, and the catastrophic effect such an experience can have on practice morale. Many GPs associate the idea of tribunal proceedings with being a "bad employer" and believe that it could never happen to them. Yet increasing numbers of GPs find themselves having to respond to tribunal applications lodged by former employees. In 1991–2 there was a 50% increase in the total number of cases going to tribunal. This included a significant increase in GP cases.

Cases can take up to a year before they are heard. Sometimes a hearing can drag on for days – five days in a recent case. Witnesses have to be called; sometimes the entire practice team, including partners, will need to attend. Practice cover will need to be organised and representation arranged. Many hours will be spent preparing witnesses and organising documents.

The two year period preceeding Mrs Jones's departure from the practice had been characterised by discord and infighting between her and other staff members and partners. Allegations had been made about verbal abuse and intimidation by her. An investigation had been carried out and several warnings had been issued to her. A procedural deficiency in one case meant that a written warning was withdrawn after the intervention of Mrs Jones's trade union representative. Further difficulties arose in the following months. Mrs Jones went on sickness absence. Her condition according to the sick note was stress. After four months, Dr Waite wrote to her expressing concern about the effect her absence was having on the practice (particularly so after Mrs Jones had been seen at several recent social functions). He requested that she undergo a medical examination so that an accurate assessment of her medical condition could be made.

Shortly afterwards the practice received a request from the local council seeking a reference on behalf of Mrs Jones. She had been made a conditional offer of employment in the Domestic Services Department at the town hall. The senior partner returned the reference form answering various questions as accurately and as truthfully as he could. The following day the practice received a letter of resignation from Mrs Jones. Dr Waite returned her P45 form as requested, together with her outstanding pay in lieu of holidays.

Two weeks later the senior partner was surprised to receive a telephone call from the local UNISON office. Apparently Mrs Jones's offer of employment had been withdrawn on the basis of an unsatisfactory reference. Mrs Jones was demanding compensation and alleged that the reference had cost her the job with the council. The practice refused. Mrs Jones lodged an application with the industrial tribunal alleging constructive dismissal. The union argued that she had been forced to resign on the grounds of the practice's behaviour; it cited the procedural inconsistencies in the earlier disciplinary procedure and the response made to her recent sickness absence. According to the union, the practice had breached the trust and confidence which should exist between employer and employee and which is implied into every contract of employment.

It took 10 months for the case to reach the tribunal. The doctors contacted the BMA for help. The BMA agreed to represent the practice. In the months before the hearing witnesses and documents were organised, negotiations took place between the BMA and UNISON with a conciliation officer from ACAS acting as an intermediary. The union indicated that Mrs Jones wanted £5000 to settle. The doctors, on advice, reckoned their chances of resisting the claim to be good, although nothing could be certain. Dr Waite had to go through files and diaries chronicling every event, no matter how insignificant, involving Mrs Jones. As the date of the hearing drew nearer the doctors and Dr Waite found it impossible to concentrate on anything else. Morale among the practice staff was low; everything seemed to depend on the outcome of the case.

On the day (after two sleepless nights) Dr Waite took his seat next to the BMA representative at the front table in the tribunal. The case took a full three days – all five partners gave evidence, as did the practice manager. After the first day, during which Mrs Jones ("the applicant") gave evidence, the doctors became downhearted. In the hands of a skilled union advocate they felt themselves somehow guilty, having unwittingly omitted certain stages of the practice disciplinary procedure, and having requested Mrs Jones who was suffering from work-related stress to undergo a medical examination.

Some relief came on the second day when the doctors had to give their evidence. On the third day all parties were on tenterhooks – both sides summed up and the tribunal members retired to reach their decision. At 16.00 the tribunal returned. According to the chairman Mrs Jones had resigned; there had been no constructive dismissal. The sense of relief for the doctors was overwhelming. The practice had waited nearly a year for confirmation that they had not acted unfairly or unreasonably. Their actions had been vindicated.

It would of course have been better if the case could have been avoided; but Mrs Jones had wanted her day in court and was playing for high stakes. Lessons were learnt; to make sure that practice disciplinary procedures were up to date and were followed to the letter, that advice should always be taken over tricky employment problems, and not to act hastily in disciplinary matters. It was indeed an experience that neither John Waite nor his partners, would ever forget and hope will never be repeated.

Facts about industrial tribunals

Increasingly, GPs are faced with the prospect of defending themselves before an industrial tribunal. Usually this follows the decision by the practice to dismiss a member of staff. The costs involved can be high; not only in financial terms but in terms of time, effort, and stress.

What are industrial tribunals? – Industrial tribunals were created as special industrial courts to provide a cheap, informal, and speedy means of adjudicating small scale employment disputes. Although these features exist there is a growing tendency towards a greater degree of formality and legalism. A tribunal is made up of a presiding chairperson, who must be a barrister or solicitor of at least seven years' standing, and two lay members drawn from both sides of industry and appointed by the Secretary of State for Employment.

How formal are tribunal proceedings? – Proceedings are regulated by the rules of procedure made by the Secretary of State. At the tribunal the chairperson is responsible for ensuring that the case is conducted in an orderly fashion and that the main strengths of each party's case have been produced in evidence. Tribunals are not bound by the same strict rules of evidence that apply in ordinary courts and should conduct the hearing "in such a manner as it considers most suitable to the clarification of the issues before it". It should also "seek to avoid formality". To ensure procedural fairness the tribunal must follow the rules of natural justice.

What is natural justice? – Basically this is the principle that justice must not only be done, but be seen to be done. Essentially, natural justice requires that:

- Both parties present their cases fully and openly
- Each party is entitled to know the case they have to meet in order to succeed

165

- Neither party be denied the right to present relevant evidence, call witnesses, or cross examine
- A tribunal act impartially and without bias.

What type of claims do industrial tribunals hear? – Although the vast majority of cases heard involve unfair dismissal or redundancy claims, tribunals have jurisdiction over many statutory provisions relating to employment matters including:

- Written statement of terms and conditions of employment
- Unauthorised deduction from wages
- Sex and race discrimination
- Pregnancy (failure to return to work)
- Equal pay claims
- Time off work (for antenatal care, public duties, trade union activities or duties, redundancy, safety representatives)
- Certain appeals under the Health and Safety at Work Act, 1994
- In 1994 industrial tribunals were given jurisdiction to hear claims by employees for breach of contract by an employer (previously these could only be heard in the civil courts). Claims before an industrial tribunal are subject to certain limitations and carry the power to award up to £25 000 in compensation.

What remedies can a tribunal award? – In the vast majority of cases when an employer loses, the tribunal orders the payment of compensation. In unfair dismissal cases the maximum award is currently £17 150, although where a re-employment or reinstatement order is not complied with this could be increased to £22 480. Higher awards are available if the reasons for dismissal are related to trade union membership or non-membership, or to a health and safety reason. Awards in cases involving race and sex discrimination are not subject to any statutory limit.

Tribunals are empowered to make:

- An order to pay compensation
- An order for re-employment – that is, an employee either to be taken back on the same terms of employment as before, or re-engage in a different job on similar terms
- A declaration.

Is there a time limit for employees to bring a claim? – Yes, in most cases. In unfair dismissal cases, for example, a complaint must be made within three months of dismissal. In other cases the time limits are between three and six months. Changes to maternity provisions introduced in October 1994 established at statutory new entitlement of 14 weeks' maternity leave period to all pregnant employees regardless or service of hours worked.

Do employees have to meet qualifying conditions? – Yes. An employee must have enough continuous service with the practice to be entitled to bring a claim. This varies with the type of claim – for example, there is a two year minimum continuous service requirement in cases involving unfair dismissal and redundancy payments. The two year qualifying period does not apply to claims arising from trade union membership, non-membership, or activities; for activities undertaken to protect the health and safety of employees; for asserting certain statutory rights; or for claims of sex and race discrimination. Part time staff now have the same rights as full time staff and are no longer subject to any "qualifying hours" requirement.

If I lose a case do I have to pay costs? – Costs might be awarded when: (a) a party persisted with a case despite a warning that it appeared to have no merit, (b) the hearing of the case has been postponed at the request of the applicant or respondent, or (c) the tribunal decides that a party has "in bringing or conducting the proceedings acted vexatiously or otherwise unreasonably". (New rules have extended this provision to include circumstances where a party has acted "abusively or disruptively".)

Do I need to be represented? – Although tribunals are supposed to be accessible and free from technicalities, research shows that your chances of winning are increased if you are represented. Because of the complexities involved and the need for advocacy skills, specialist representation would undoubtedly help your case. You may be represented by someone of your choice including a solicitor or a friend (a GP BMA member is entitled to BMA representation).

Are tribunals on the increase? – Yes. A record 73 000 cases went before tribunals in 1993 – an increase of more than 150% from five years before. This has in some areas lead to a huge backlog and increased costs.

How do I defend a claim? – On receipt of a complaint (form IT1), the tribunal sends the respondent a notice of appearance (form IT3) asking for "sufficient details to show the grounds on which you intend to resist the application". Always seek advice before completing this. Over 60% of cases are settled by conciliation (arranged by ACAS) or withdrawn before the hearing. On the IT3 you should list facts that are uncontroversial and that you are confident about. It is a good idea to "plead in the alternative" which allows you to argue on several fronts. In constructive dismissal cases, for instance, you may argue that the employee was not dismissed, but "in the alternative" that he or she was dismissed for a fair and reasonable reason (misconduct).

What preliminary work is needed? – Cases are not necessarily won on skill in advocacy, but more often on the preparatory work prior to the hearing. The outcome of a case is usually established by a tribunal "on a balance of probabilities". To help establish the tribunal's view in your favour, relevant facts should be gathered from documents in your possession, by requesting further particulars and documents from the other side, and by calling witnesses. Documents should be assembled as a bundle, for use by the tribunal. Pages should be numbered in the top right hand corner and sent to the tribunal before the day of the hearing. In dismissal cases, essential documents to include are the contract of employment, job description, disciplinary procedure, record of disciplinary investigations or hearings, copies of written warnings or recorded verbal warnings, letters of dismissal or resignation, and so on. Tribunals prefer to hear direct from the principal protagonists involved, so witnesses are important. Only witnesses who can help establish the essential facts of the case should be called. Make sure witnesses are briefed on what will happen.

What happens at the tribunal? – Cases are usually heard within 20 weeks of receipt of the IT1 and normally last about a day. Attempts to settle often continue up to the hearing. The opening party is usually the one who has to discharge the burden of proof. Where a dismissal is disputed, the applicant must prove that he or she has been dismissed. Once this has been established, it is for the respondent to show the reasons for it. The tribunal must then decide whether the employer acted "reasonably".

How will the case be presented and decided? – An opening statement is not necessary, but you can ask to give a summary. A closing statement is important to highlight contradictions in the other side's case and draw attention to unchallenged evidence.

The tribunal usually retires for a short period and returns with a verbal decision. The written decision will be sent later. A "reserved decision" means the tribunal wishes to take more time

---

Sequence of events at industrial tribunal hearing

- First party makes opening statement, if allowed, and presents witnesses – who give evidence "in chief", are cross examined, and then re-examined
- Second party presents witnesses as above and makes a closing statement
- First party makes closing statement
- The tribunal retires to reach a decision

---

to consider. Once the decision is signed by a chairman or chairwoman, it is final and is entered into the register of the Central Office of the Industrial Tribunals.

28 Avoiding age discrimination at work – a time for change

"Too old"; "past it"; "over the hill". Comments such as these are often made about candidates for jobs, staff being considered for promotion, or those selected for early retirement or redundancy. Agism is deeply rooted at work and in society generally. In employment age-related assumptions about a person's skills, abilities, and work orientation are made throughout their career (see box 1). Yet in most occupations there is little correlation between age and performance. Commenting on an EC policy of only recruiting workers under the age of 35, former Employment Minister Michael Forsyth said that the use of blanket and arbitrary age restrictions in employment could not be justified and those who imposed them would lose out on the skills and experience of older workers.

The government has set up a special advisory committee to tackle age discrimination in employment and to advise employers on how to eliminate it. Stephen Ward, vice president of the Institute of Personnel Management and a member of its advisory committee, states that "age is never relevant to an appointment process. People mix up age with experience. It is perfectly legitimate to demand that candidates have a minimum level of experience, but it is totally unfair to assume that somebody at 20 is less mature than somebody at 40".

170

Box 1 – Age discrimination and the employment cycle

Arbitrary age discrimination can be overt or covert and occurs directly and indirectly at all stages of the employment cycle, including:

- Job definition

- Job or person specifications

- Recruitment procedures, including advertising, sorting and sifting application forms and CVs, shortlisting, selection interviewing, and selection decisions

- Training, including induction, career development, skills, training, and counselling

- Appraisal

- Promotion

- Pay and remuneration packages

- Retention, redundancy, termination, and retirement.

[*Source: Age and Employment* An IPM Statement. Institute of Personnel Management, 1991].

What is age discrimination?

Age discrimination is the stereotyping of people, on the basis of their age, which prevents the proper assessment of an individual's ability, skills, and experience. Similar to race and sex discrimination, it is arbitrary and is often the result of ignorance and prejudice. It can affect the young as well as older members of society. At work, age discrimination leads to the ineffective use of human resources (see box 2). A recent survey by the Equal Opportunities Commission showed that 25% of job adverts quoted arbitrary age limits. Employers who set arbitrary age limits miss out on a rich variety of skills, experience, and commitment that older workers can bring to a job. Generalisations and negative beliefs about older employees are rarely justifiable. Indeed, most studies show that age is an unreliable predictor of performance at work. Research has shown that older employees are often more productive, have fewer accidents and less absenteeism, and show a greater commitment to a job than their younger colleagues.

Box 2 – Key facts about age and age discrimination

- Age is a poor predictor of job performance
- It is misleading to equate physical and mental ability with age
- More people are living active, healthy lives as they get older
- There is an increasing number of older workers in the labour market
- Age is rarely a genuine employment criterion
- Society's attitudes may encourage compliance with out-moded personnel practice regarding recruitment, promotion, training, redundancy, and retirement
- Reduced self confidence, self esteem, and motivation, together with loss or reduction of financial independence for individuals and their dependents, are some of the harmful effects of age discrimination.

[*Source: Age and Employment.* An IPM Statement. Institute of Personnel Managers, 1991].

The greying workforce

At times of economic recession older employees tend to be early victims. Early retirement and redundancy schemes generally favour younger workers. The economic recessions in the early 1980s and 1990s showed how the economic activity rate for men aged 55-64 fell dramatically.

However, as the post war baby boomers get older and concern about the demographic time bomb grows, age discrimination is emerging as a major public policy issue. There is growing pressure for legislation along similar lines to existing race and sex discrimination legislation. So far in parliament there have been several unsuccessful attempts to introduce legislation prohibiting the use of upper age limits in recruitment advertising. The government has so far ruled out legislation on the issue in preference to trying to persuade employers to abandon agist practices.

Experience from abroad

In Canada it is unlawful to deprive individuals of employment opportunities on grounds of age. Similarly, in the US legislation has been passed that prohibits arbitrary age discrimination. It is unlawful for American employers to "limit, segregate, or classify an employee in any way which deprives that employee of job opportunities or adversely affects employment status because of their age".

In the EC, France is the only member state that has legislation protecting older workers. Two reports calling for action on agism have already been placed before the European parliament, although progress has been slow, particularly given the British government's reluctance to legislate on the issue.

Age restrictions and current British law

No express legislation currently prevents discrimination at work on grounds of age. As a general rule, age limits are therefore usually lawful. The only exception is where an age limit can be shown to have an adverse proportional impact on grounds of either sex or race and cannot be shown as justifiable. For example in one case an employer who required job applicants to be under 28 was found to have discriminated against women because in reality it is mainly women who leave the job market to assume family and child rearing responsibilities and return later. It is unlawful to specify separate retirement ages for men and women under the Sex Discrimination Act, 1986. Employment may continue beyond 60 or 65 subject to the provisions of the employment contract. Several employers have not yet altered their terms and conditions of service to reflect the 1986 act and are vulnerable to claims if their terms of service specify different retirement ages according to sex. If there is a conflict, or no common retirement age is specified for male and female employees, the assumption is that the normal retirement age is 65. When employers allow members to work beyond the normal retirement age it must apply equally to all employees regardless of sex.

Action to be taken

The prevention of age discrimination involves raising the level of awareness of the issues through information and education. A number of employers, particularly in the public sector and local government, are developing and promoting a positive approach to best employment practice as a means of changing attitudes about age and age related criteria in employment. A series of recommendations and guidelines for all employers is slowly emerging. Clearly these won't necessarily be appropriate to all employment situations, and some will need the involvement of government, educators, and others.

In the year 2000 there will be 1·8 million more 35-40 year olds at work and 1 in 3 of the labour force will be over 40. Life expectancy (now 77 for women and 71 for men) continues to rise. The employment of older workers has become a crucial issue. Britain faces a substantial labour shortage, which will continue

---

Box 3 - Organisational policies - checklist for action

- All equal opportunity statements should include an explicit reference to age and should be well publicised and given to job applicants

- All personnel policies and procedures, and terms and conditions of employment, should be reviewed

- Equal opportunity training programmes should make specific reference to age discrimination, and provide managers and other employers with a means of reducing its incidence

- A monitoring system should be set up to measure progress

- Career development schemes should make sure that current policy and practice take account of older workers' needs. Positive encouragement should be given to older workers and those returning to work

- Age limits should be removed from all recruitment advertising. Consideration should be given to removing the date of birth from job application forms

- New patterns of work should be explored to see if they help to assess and retain those with the skills the organisation requires. (Career break schemes, job sharing, working times which will take account of school holidays, flexitime, and flexible retirement arrangements)

- Pension schemes should be examined to see if the current ages at which retirement takes place should give way to greater flexibility with the option to continue to work after state retirement age

---

into the next century. The government has recognised this and, although it refuses to legislate, it has set about raising the awareness of employers and managers on the issue. All practices should be encouraged to base their personnel policies, including recruitment and training, on job related criteria (skills, qualifications, potential, competence, etc) rather than rely on arbitrary and unjustifiable notions about age.

29 Contemplating redundancy

Of all the business decisions facing practice managers and GPs, few can be as traumatic as declaring staff redundant. Not many practices will have experienced the upheaval and trauma involved. With the NHS reforms and the greater emphasis on competition and efficiency, together with the additional powers given to FHSA, practices may have to look very closely at their staffing levels in future and revise them in line with the new NHS environment. For individuals affected, redundancy can be disastrous financially as well as psychologically. Employers need to consider the issue sensitively and in line with good practice.

What is redundancy?

In law an employee is redundant if an entire business or part of a business is closed, or if fewer people are needed to do the work available. A practice's requirements for fewer staff to do the available work may occur for one of several reasons such as:

- Decreasing levels of business
- Reorganisation of working practices or working hours
- The introduction of new technology (such as computerisation)
- Putting work out to contractors

Handling redundancies: good practice

When faced with a potential redundancy employers should follow established good practice (see box). Failure to follow such

---

Redundancy procedures should involve:

- Giving as much warning as possible to staff concerned
- Consulting staff and, when appropriate, trade union representatives to try to minimise the need for redundancies
- Minimising the hardship concerned and acting fairly
- Considering alternatives, such as the availability of other work in the practice
- Establishing fair and objective criteria in selecting individuals for redundancy

---

procedures could result in a tribunal finding the redundancy unfair.

Consultation

The requirement to consult is obviously a matter of good industrial relations practice and also gives all concerned the opportunity to share the problem and explore options. Consultation should take place at the earliest opportunity. There is a statutory duty on an employer to consult trade union representatives if the employer recognises the union concerned for negotiation purposes.

Avoiding or minimising redundancies

When faced with potential redundancies practices should take all possible steps to minimise and, if possible, to avoid compulsory redundancies. Before contemplating them, the following alternatives should be considered:

- Natural wastage
- Voluntary redundancy
- Curbing recruitment
- Limiting the use of temporary staff
- Recalling any work that has been subcontracted
- Looking at the possibility of early voluntary retirement
- Reducing any overtime working
- Reducing hours of work in the practice.

177

Selecting staff for redundancy

When selecting people for redundancy a practice must apply criteria that are objective, precisely defined, and capable of being applied consistently in an independent way. For example, typical criteria might be length of service, attendance records, disciplinary records, experience, and capability (that is, the skills, experience, and aptitude of the employee). Alternatively, selection might be based on the last in first out principle. The dismissal of an employee for redundancy will be unfair if the selection criterion (a) breaches a customary or agreed procedure, (b) relates to a trade union reason, or (c) discriminates on grounds of race or sex. Furthermore, a dismissal may be unfair when the reason, or principal reason, is redundancy but the circumstances apply equally to other employees who have not been selected.

When the application of selection criteria results in the loss of an employee with important skills or knowledge which the practice needs to retain then the redundancy can be transferred to another employee. This process is called "bumping". Care should be taken, because tribunals will look closely at the reasons for selecting the "non-redundant" employee for dismissal.

What are the costs involved?

An employee dismissed by reason of redundancy may be entitled to a statutory redundancy payment. To qualify, an employee must have been continuously employed for two years or more and be aged under 65, or under normal retirement age if that is lower than 65. Employment below the age of 18 does not count towards continuous employment.

Redundancy payments are calculated by taking the number of years of employment in each of the age ranges given in the table and multiplying by the appropriate number of weeks' pay. Employment beyond 20 years is not counted so the maximum payment is $20 \times 1 \cdot 5 = 30$ weeks' pay. There is a maximum level of weekly pay, currently £205. Payment is reduced by 1/12 for each month beyond the age of 64.

A claim for redundancy compensation must be made to an industrial tribunal or by writing to the employer within six months. The right to compensation is lost if the employer offers "suitable" alternative employment and the employee "unrea-

TABLE Ready reckoner for calculating the number of weeks' pay due

Service (years) → Age (years) ↓	2	3	4	5	6	7	8	9	10	11	12	13	14	15	16	17	18	19	20
20	1	1	1	1	-														
21	1	1½	1½	1½	1½	-													
22	1	1½	2	2	2	2	-												
23	1½	2	2½	3	3	3	3	-											
24	2	2½	3	3½	4	4	4	4	-										
25	2	3	3½	4	4½	5	5	5	5	-									
26	2	3	4	4½	5	5½	6	6	6	6	-								
27	2	3	4	5	5½	6	6½	7	7	7	7	-							
28	2	3	4	5	6	6½	7	7½	8	8	8	8	-						
29	2	3	4	5	6	7	7½	8	8½	9	9	9	9	-					
30	2	3	4	5	6	7	8	8½	9	9½	10	10	10	10	-				
31	2	3	4	5	6	7	8	9	9½	10	10½	11	11	11	11	-			
32	2	3	4	5	6	7	8	9	10	10½	11	11½	12	12	12	12	-		
33	2	3	4	5	6	7	8	9	10	11	11½	12	12½	13	13	13	13	-	
34	2	3	4	5	6	7	8	9	10	11	12	12½	13	13½	14	14	14	14	-
35	2	3	4	5	6	7	8	9	10	11	12	13	13½	14	14½	15	15	15	15
36	2	3	4	5	6	7	8	9	10	11	12	13	14	14½	15	15½	16	16	16
37	2	3	4	5	6	7	8	9	10	11	12	13	14	15	15½	16	16½	17	17
38	2	3	4	5	6	7	8	9	10	11	12	13	14	15	16	16½	17	17½	18
39	2	3	4	5	6	7	8	9	10	11	12	13	14	15	16	17	17½	18	18½
40	2	3	4	5	6	7	8	9	10	11	12	13	14	15	16	17	18	18½	19
41	2	3	4	5	6	7	8	9	10	11	12	13	14	15	16	17	18	19	19½
42	2½	3½	4½	5½	6½	7½	8½	9½	10½	11½	12½	13½	14½	15½	16½	17½	18½	19½	20½
43	3	4	5	6	7	8	9	10	11	12	13	14	15	16	17	18	19	20	21
44	3	4½	5½	6½	7½	8½	9½	10½	11½	12½	13½	14½	15½	16½	17½	18½	19½	20½	21½
45	3	4½	6	7	8	9	10	11	12	13	14	15	16	17	18	19	20	21	22
46	3	4½	6	7½	8½	9½	10½	11½	12½	13½	14½	15½	16½	17½	18½	19½	20½	21½	22½
47	3	4½	6	7½	9	10	11	12	13	14	15	16	17	18	19	20	21	22	23
48	3	4½	6	7½	9	10½	11½	12½	13½	14½	15½	16½	17½	18½	19½	20½	21½	22½	23½
49	3	4½	6	7½	9	10½	12	13	14	15	16	17	18	19	20	21	22	23	24
50	3	4½	6	7½	9	10½	12	13½	14½	15½	16½	17½	18½	19½	20½	21½	22½	23½	24½
51	3	4½	6	7½	9	10½	12	13½	15	16	17	18	19	20	21	22	23	24	25
52	3	4½	6	7½	9	10½	12	13½	15	16½	17½	18½	19½	20½	21½	22½	23½	24½	25½
53	3	4½	6	7½	9	10½	12	13½	15	16½	18	19	20	21	22	23	24	25	26
54	3	4½	6	7½	9	10½	12	13½	15	16½	18	19½	20½	21½	22½	23½	24½	25½	26½
55	3	4½	6	7½	9	10½	12	13½	15	16½	18	19½	21	22	23	24	25	26	27
56	3	4½	6	7½	9	10½	12	13½	15	16½	18	19½	21	22½	23½	24½	25½	26½	27½
57	3	4½	6	7½	9	10½	12	13½	15	16½	18	19½	21	22½	24	25	26	27	28
58	3	4½	6	7½	9	10½	12	13½	15	16½	18	19½	21	22½	24	25½	26½	27½	28½
59	3	4½	6	7½	9	10½	12	13½	15	16½	18	19½	21	22½	24	25½	27	28	29
60	3	4½	6	7½	9	10½	12	13½	15	16½	18	19½	21	22½	24	25½	27	28½	29½
61	3	4½	6	7½	9	10½	12	13½	15	16½	18	19½	21	22½	24	25½	27	28½	30
62	3	4½	6	7½	9	10½	12	13½	15	16½	18	19½	21	22½	24	25½	27	28½	30
63	3	4½	6	7½	9	10½	12	13½	15	16½	18	19½	21	22½	24	25½	27	28½	30
64	3	4½	6	7½	9	10½	12	13½	15	16½	18	19½	21	22½	24	25½	27	28½	30

sonably refuses it". If the terms of any new employment offered differ from those for the old job the employee is entitled to a trial period of four weeks without losing his entitlement to claim redundancy compensation. Employees under notice of redundancy and who qualify for a statutory redundancy payment are entitled to take reasonable time off to look for other work or to arrange training.

Redundancy, as well as being a traumatic process, is a legal maze. It needs to be handled sensitively and with due regard to existing good practice and reasonable procedures. Practices making staff redundant should always seek expert advice. Copies of the ACAS advisory booklet on how to handle redundancies are available free from ACAS offices.

Index

General Practice books from the BMJ Publishing Group

CHANGE AND TEAMWORK IN PRIMARY CARE
Edited by Mike Pringle

General practice is now at the centre of the health service and this book addresses the vital challenges confronting those working in it. In the first part experts describe with real examples the skills required for managing change and in the second the tasks and relationships within the new primary health care teams are examined.

"In a time of unprecedented and unrelenting change of primary care, this is a very welcome book."
Health Education Journal

ISBN 0 7279 0779 4   120 pages

DOCTORS, DILEMMAS, DECISIONS
Ben Essex

This first book on decision making in general practice provides, using over 220 real life cases, a logical system of analysing typical problems and producing practical, ethically acceptable solutions. It covers the full range, including diagnosis, management, goals, follow up, outcome, prevention, and practice organisation.

"Opens up the whole of the basis for decisions and dilemmas for doctors."
Health Service Journal

ISBN 0 7279 0859 6   350 pages

EMPLOYING STAFF *Fifth edition*
Norman Ellis

Written specifically for general practice, this brief guide provides information on employment law. This fifth edition includes the latest developments regarding maternity leave, health and safety regulations, contract of employment – and causes of concern such as protecting staff from risk of violence and ensuring confidentiality of patient records.

"No practice in the country should be without it."
Journal of the Royal College of General Practitioners

ISBN 0 7279 0838 3   152 pages

188

THE FUTURE OF GENERAL PRACTICE

General practitioners have recently experienced dramatic changes in their working conditions as a result of government policy. This book discusses what general practice should be and how it should be funded. Topics at the heart of the debate include research, audit, list sizes, fundholding, and education.

"Should be incorporated in the prescribed list for training practices."
Journal of Epidemiology and Community Health

ISBN 0 7279 0316 0   116 pages

RIGHTS AND RESPONSIBILITIES OF DOCTORS
Second edition

This popular book provides a practical guide to the law as it affects members of the medical profession. Topics include: consent; medical malpractice; confidentiality; medical records; death; drugs.

ISBN 0 7279 0753 0   226 pages

For further details of these books and our full range of titles write to Marketing Department, BMJ Publishing Group, BMA House, Tavistock Square, London WC1H 9JR or telephone Diana Chapple on 0171 383 6541.

189